GIBBY

BY BILL IDELSON

GIBBY
© 2006 Bill Idelson

All rights reserved.

No part of this book may be reproduced in any form or by any means, electronic, mechanical, digital, photocopying or recording, except for the inclusion in a review, without permission in writing from the the publisher.

PUBLISHED IN THE USA BY:

BearManor Media
PO Box 71426
Albany, GA 31708
www.BearManorMedia.com

LIBRARY OF CONGRESS CATALOGING-IN-PUBLICATION DATA:

Idelson, Billy.
 Gibby / by Bill Idelson.
   p. cm.
 ISBN-13: 978-1-59393-059-2
 1. Winkler, Gibby. 2. World War, 1939-1945--Aerial operations, American. 3. United
States. Navy--Airmen--Training of. 4. World War, 1939-1945--Campaigns--Pacific Area. 5.
Fighter pilots--United States--Biography. I. Title.

D790.33.W56I34 2006
940.54'4973092--dc22
 [B]
                              2006021166

Printed in the United States.

Cover Art and Design by Howie Idelson.

Interior Design and Layout by Valerie Thompson.

Chapter One

His mother and father did not talk to each other for forty years. Sometimes Gibby would awaken in the wee hours to angry shouts and the sound of chairs breaking in the kitchen, but no talking. His father was home. They lived in a suburb of Chicago, a "wet" suburb, which meant that you could get a drink there. They were surrounded by "dry" suburbs, which meant, of course, that you couldn't get a drink there.

His father was a tough guy, for a Jew. Barely five-foot-two, Ben was raised in the seamy part of NYC. He had carried sides of beef on his shoulder for his father, a butcher, during the day, and fought in clubs at night. Now he owned a bar and got alcohol in twenty-gallon tins from the Capone mob, and carried a .38 in his overcoat pocket for the drive home at night.

Ben manufactured his merchandise in a locked room in the basement, and Gibby helped him. Bourbon was alcohol, distilled water and amber coloring. Gin was alcohol, distilled water and juniper flavoring. Gibby, with a hand-operated stamping machine, put a Seagram's label on the whiskey and a Gordon's label on the gin. Ben got a dollar a shot for each.

They lived in a German neighborhood. When Ben first tried to buy a house there, the neighbors circulated a petition to keep the family out, and Ben had to buy the place under a gentile customer's name. But the resentment, though hidden, was almost palpable, and followed Gibby everywhere. It was especially intensified because it was Prohibition and Ben was making a good deal more money than his factory-worker neighbors and there were sneering glances that said, "Leave it to the Jews to make money, even when it's illegal." Of course, Ben had expenses. There were generous bribes to the police chief, and thoughtful Christmas gift to Mr. Capone and his associates.

Ben got home at about 3:00 a.m., and back to work at ten, so it was seldom Gibby saw his dad unless he visited the bar. He loved the place. The rednecks filled the stools at the bar and there was a delicious free lunch at the opposite wall: Oysters on the half-shell, clams on the half-shell, a turkey, a corned beef and a boiled tongue, with plenty of Ben's secret seafood sauce, German mustard and all kinds of bread. Second-hand smoke filled the place. When Gibby came in, his father always gave him the same greeting: "Whatd'ya want? A drink or a cigar?" Gibby always took the cigar and was probably the only ten-year-old who smoked cigars in that part of the country.

But, to be honest, there were other times when he saw his father. Once, Ben took Gibby fishing at Lake Zurich, and Gibby was so thrilled with the experience he became an avid fisherman for the rest of his life. And they usually went to the fights about twice a week, where Ben knew people, having managed two fighters himself.

However, Gibby always felt that he was a disappointment to his father. Ben had mentioned at times, to people at the bar, in Gibby's hearing, that his son had been raised by "women," implying that the boy was not as red-blooded as he would have liked. After all, Ben had once fought "Terrible Terry McGovern" when they were both teenagers, and had a scar on his chin to prove it.

Gibby was in the backyard, playing with his dog, when Della, his sister, called out the window: "Hon, could you come in here? I want to ask you something." Gibby threw the stick one last time and went in the house. "Listen," she said, "I'm taking some of the kids to WGN for an audition. Would you like to come too?"

"I don't know. Maybe."

"You have to wear a clean shirt."

Gibby changed his shirt and got into the car with three other boys— Della's students. Della had graduated from Sherwood Music School, majoring in Drama, and though she harbored a secret ambition to become a professional actress herself, she now occupied her time with teaching kids to act.

On the way downtown, she explained the situation. "WGN is doing the *Tribune* comics on the radio . . . ."

"Yeah," said one of the kids, "they got **Little Orphan Annie** and *Harold Teen* every night."

The other boys looked at him enviously. "You got a radio?" asked one.

"Yeah. A big one. It's great."

"We're getting one for Christmas," said another.

"The guy next door's got a crystal set," said Gibby. "He made it himself."
"They're no good. You can't get anything."
"No? Last night he opened the window and got Chilly." (Chile)
Only one of them laughed. A Geography whiz, probably.
"Well, they're gonna do ***Gasoline Alley***," said Della. "You boys are going to try out for "Skeezix."
"Wow!"

WGN was in the Drake Hotel. They went in and the kids looked around in awe, never having been in a classy hotel before. The radio station was on the top floor. They were ushered into a sort of meeting room where there were about a dozen kids standing and sitting around. Della went over and spoke to a guy in a suit who seemed to be in charge, then came back to her little group, carrying scripts. "They're going to start soon. You'll go into the studio one at a time and read with somebody." She handed out the scripts and showed them the page they would read from.

Gibby was bored. He looked at the lines and they seemed dumb. And it seemed to take forever for the kids to go into the studio and come out. And, of course, his bunch was last to go in.

But finally, it was Gibby's turn.

There was a woman waiting for him at a microphone. She didn't look at him. There was a large glass window to his right, with several men seated behind it. A man's voice came over the speaker: "O.K. Your name, please."

"Gibby . . . ." He had a frog in his throat and cleared it. "Gibby Winkler."

"O.K. You've looked at the lines?"

"Yeah."

"Good. Miss Bennett will read with you. She has the first line. Go ahead."

Miss Bennett read her line and Gibby read his.

"Closer to the mike, Gibby," said the voice on the speaker.

"O.K." He got closer to the mike and they read the whole page.

"All right," said the speaker. "Not bad. How would you like to play Skeezix?"

"O.K., I guess," said Gibby.

"You wouldn't be happy about it?"

"Oh, yeah. I would. I guess."

There was a laugh from the guy behind the glass. "Well, if you're it, we'll call you."

"O.K. Thanks."

He went back into the waiting room. "How did it go?" asked Della.

"I don't know. I made a couple of mistakes . . . ."

"Oh, that's O.K."

She drove the other kids home and then brought Gibby back to the house. Their mother had dinner ready. Della and Gibby told her about the audition, and she just nodded, not particularly impressed.

"What if I get the part?" asked Gibby.

"Well, I wouldn't get my hopes up. They've auditioned about a hundred kids," said Della.

But about a week later, when Gibby came home from school, Della threw her arms around him, laughing like a fool. "You got it!" she cried. "You're Skeezix!"

He couldn't believe it. "God. What do I do now?"

"They'll call again tomorrow and tell you all about it."

Of course, he told his friends and the news spread quickly. The response at school varied. The teachers seemed impressed, as were some of the girls. The boys' response ran mostly to derision. It seemed sort of a sissy thing to them, although Gibby sometimes sensed a bit of envy.

A reporter from the village newspaper went to the bar and talked to Ben, and his father revealed that Gibby would be earning fifty dollars a week, which, in the prevailing Depression, was about twice what most men, lucky enough to have a job, were earning. More snide glances and sneering comments.

And there was more downside. He was picked up at school when classes were over and driven by one of his father's bartenders, along with his mother, down to the radio station. His afternoons were no longer free. No more baseball, no more football, no more hanging out. His father's attitude was also ambiguous. To some extent, he mirrored the feelings of the boys at school. Although he seemed proud of his son, there was also a sense that he considered it not one of the most masculine things to do. In general, it added to Gibby's sense of isolation and difference from the other kids he knew; what he wanted most was to be just like them.

Chapter Two

Around the studios, it was interesting at times. He saw the girl who played Little Orphan Annie, her pal Joe Corntassel, Harold Teen, Easy Aces, some of the well-known announcers, and even a movie star or two who were in town and at the station for an interview. But the radio show itself didn't always hold his interest. Sometimes, during the program, his mind would wander and he would miss a cue. His colleagues put it down to inexperience, and weren't too hard on him, but the novelty of his situation was wearing thin and he wasn't too disappointed when the show was canceled after thirteen weeks.

He told his mother and Della that he really didn't enjoy being on the radio and that he wasn't anxious to do it anymore. But his career refused to end that easily. There was a call asking for him to come down to WGN for a talk with Pat Donahue, manager of the station. Gibby didn't want to go, but his mother made it clear that refusing the chance to bring a little extra money into the house in these times was a luxury they couldn't afford.

Pat was an Irishman with a round face and a little mustache like Hitler. "I do a show every afternoon for Big Three Oatmeal," he said. "Kids send in the labels off the Big Three boxes with their names and addresses on the back. I read the names, and at the end of the week I draw one out of a hat and that kid gets a prize. Have you heard the show, by any chance?"

"We don't have a radio. We're gonna get one, though."

"I see. You should get one, soon."

"I know."

"Anyway, the sponsor thinks it would be good to have a kid on with me, to read the labels and pick the winner at the end of the week. I thought of you."

"Uh-huh."

"And also I read a story to them every day. You could read the story."

"Uh-huh."

"What do you think?"

"Uh . . . I guess so . . . ."

"So, we'll start tomorrow. The show goes on at five. Be here at four."

"O.K."

They were in a tiny studio, not more than eight-by-ten feet, sitting side-by-side at a table with a goose-neck mike hanging between them, a gunnysack full of labels next to Pat. He introduced Gibby to the audience as his new assistant and they began reading the labels alternately. When they got one that mentioned a birthday, Pat rang a bell that stood beside him.

Then he said, after about ten minutes into the show: "O.K., now Gibby is going to read you a story about a princess who gets lost in the woods." He shoved a book over to Gibby, put his finger on the place, got up and walked out. Gibby began to read the story, which he had never seen before, painfully aware that he was on live radio, all alone, naked before the world. He read, on and on, coming toward the end of the story and wondering if his partner was ever coming back. He read slower and slower, drawling out the words. What was he going to do? When he finished, would he start another story? It was like being alone on a raft, in a sea full of sharks. He could feel the sweat coming out on his forehead. His voice shook. The last few lines sounded like he was eighty years old.

Suddenly the door opened and Pat strode in, his face flushed and a smile on his lips. "Wasn't that great?" he said, sliding into his seat. "I love that story. Don't you, Gibby?"

"Yeah," croaked Gibby as the theme music played on a speaker.

The mystery of Pat's absence from the studio while Gibby read the daily story to the kids was revealed when he overheard some of the studio personnel gossiping about it in the hall. "… sure, he goes out to have a drink. He can't go for half an hour without a belt."

Pat came up with another job for him. Every Saturday afternoon the two of them would appear on stage at a movie theater in the area and read the Sunday comics to the kids. Another day shot, when he could be having fun with his friends. But this too came to an end after a few months when the show was cancelled.

Now Gibby declared, in no uncertain terms, that he was through with radio, no matter what. He absolutely would accept no more jobs, even if they paid a million dollars. He was through, understand? Done! Finished! Kaput! No more radio!

He went back to being a kid again; playing after school, riding his bike, tormenting girls, roller skating—all the things that made life worthwhile.

Chapter Three

One day, his mother announced, hesitantly, that there had been a call from NBC . . . about a job . . . and she had accepted.

Gibby hit the roof. No! He wouldn't go! Hadn't he told her, and everybody else, that he had retired? No! No! Call them back! Explain it to them! He was through! No more radio!

He ranted and raved for nearly an hour. Then his mother said quietly that the job was for only four days. Four days! And she had given her word. Four days was certainly not going to kill him. "Please! Be a good boy and don't make your poor mother into a liar . . ."

Exhausted, Gibby at last said O.K.—but only for four days. O.K.?

He and his mother arrived at NBC at 7:00 A.M., the time scheduled for rehearsal. The nineteenth-floor lobby was empty except for a man and woman seated on the hard black benches meant for visitors. They smiled when they saw him.

"Here's Clay!" said the woman. The man stood up to shake his hand.

"I'm Jeanette," said the woman. "Bess."

"And I'm Bert. Nick."

They greeted Gibby's mother and shook hands with her. She went and sat down at a bench apart from them.

In spite of himself, Gibby had a positive impression of these people. They seemed sincere and really friendly.

Then a middle-aged man came in from the hall. The introductions were made again and this guy seemed friendly too, but in a more subdued way. He was Edwin Mercer, program manager of NBC in Chicago. He looked distinguished and no bull. He was also going to direct the show. Mercer sat down at the reception desk, facing them.

"Gibby," he said. "Welcome. I don't suppose you've heard this show on the air."

"We don't have a radio yet."

"Uh-huh. Well, you're probably on your way to school when it's broadcast, anyway. Eight-thirty in the morning. The show started ten days ago with just the two characters—Nick and Bess. Then we decided we needed a kid. Now the way we accomplished this—Bess has an old friend who lives a couple hundred miles away, and they are in bad shape financially, with two kids, a boy and a girl, and a husband out of work. Now, they can't really take care of the kids, so they ask if Nick and Bess could take care of the boy until things pick up. Understand?"

"For four days?"

"What?"

"They're going to take care of him for four days?"

"Oh, no. There's no specified time. We'll see how it goes . . ."

Gibby stole a look at his mother. She was looking into space.

They rehearsed until 8:25, then went over and pushed open the double set of heavy doors and entered studio "B," which was one of the large studios used mostly for musical programs. A blast of peppy, early morning music assailed them. It came from a twenty-piece orchestra that occupied the center of the room. Walter Blaufuss was up in front on a small platform, waving away uncritically with his baton, turning to nod and smile to the actors coming in. Against the far wall was a square, beige cloth tent, open on the one side that dramatic shows used to avoid a boomy sound. Inside the tent, there were two standing microphones, one for Bert and Jeanette, and a shorter one for Gibby.

The actors made their way to the tent as Walter drove to a big finish. The announcer wrapped up *Morning Serenade*, rang his chimes and the orchestra broke into the *Nick and Bess* theme: "Oh, You Beautiful Doll." The announcer introduced the show and they were on the air.

The show was about the boy, Vic, being in the house, having arrived the night before. Bess wakes up Nick, telling him that during the night she heard the boy crying. She suggests that they try to amuse him, keep him busy in some way —

NICK: OKAY, KIDDO. HEY, LET'S SNEAK INTO HIS ROOM WHEELING THAT BICYCLE. THAT'LL CHEER HIM UP, I'LL BET MY SHIRT. HE HASN'T GOT A BICYCLE, HAS HE?

BESS: NO . . . I ASKED HIM LAST NIGHT. HE NEVER HAD ONE, HE SAID. BUT I GATHERED HE'D LIKE TO HAVE ONE.

Nick: (*Chuckling*) Let's go!

Bess: Wait, Nick. He wouldn't want us to know he's been crying. You go get the bicycle. I'll knock on his door.

Nick: (*On his way*) Sure. Golly, don't know when I've been up this early before . . . ain't hardly daylight yet. I . . .

SFX: Knock

Bess: (*Softly*) Vic.

(*Little Pause*)

Vic: (*Inside*) Yes'm

SFX: Open door

Bess: Good morning, Vic.

Vic: Good morning.

Bess: Did you sleep well, Vic?

Vic: Yes, ma'm. Thank you.

(*Little Pause*)

Bess: Was the . . . was the bed comfortable?

Vic: Yes, ma'm. Thank you.

(*Little Pause*)

Bess: Is that a scar on your arm, Vic?

Vic: Yeah . . . got hit with a stick that had a nail in it.

Bess: Uh-huh.

Vic: Got one on this arm too. Vaccination.

BESS: Uh-huh.

VIC: You got a vaccination scar?

BESS: Yes.

VIC: Lemme see it.

BESS: See.

VIC: It's bigger 'n mine. Red Williams got a bigger one than yours even.

BESS: Has he?

VIC: Yeah . . . he made his bigger with a piece of glass. (*Laughs and is joined by Bess*) He got a lickin' for it.

BESS: Did he?

VIC: (*Polite again*) Yes, ma'm.

(*Little Pause*)

BESS: Want me to help you with your tie?

VIC: No, ma'm.

(*Little Pause*)

BESS: You're short a tooth in front, aren't you?

VIC: Uh-huh, pulled it out myself.

BESS: Gee, I'll bet it hurt.

VIC: Yea, a bit. Got 'nother one coming in though. See?

BESS: Uh-huh.

VIC: Got a tooth gone in the back too. Back here.

Chapter Three   11

(*Talks a little with his finger in his mouth, unintelligibly, of course. They both laugh*)

Nick: (*Coming in*) Good morning, young fella.

Vic: Good morning, sir.

Nick: How'd ya sleep?

Vic: Fine, thank you, sir.

Nick: That's good. Gosh, I'm all out of breath, Bess. Just ran around the block forty times.

Bess: Did you, Nick?

Nick: Yeah. D'you ever run around the block forty times, Vic?

Vic: No, sir.

Nick: I hadda run around the block this morning. Y'see, I got a watch that doesn't go very good . . . so I hadda run around the block forty times or it'd stop.

Vic: (*Laughing*) Aw, you're foolin'.

(*All three laugh heartily*)

Bess: I'll run down and get us something to eat. Are you hungry, Vic?

Vic: Yes, ma'm. A . . . don't go to no trouble.

Bess: Why, you darling. Listen, I'm going down and make some wheat cakes. Like wheat cakes?

Vic: Pancakes?

Bess: Yes. Pancakes.

Vic: Yes, I like 'em.

Nick: Wait a minute, Bess. I was trying to figure out that bicycle I bought and it don't fit me.

Bess: It don't fit you?

Nick: No, it's too small. Don't know what on earth I'm gonna do with it. The man won't take it back now that I've used it. Wonder if I could sell it to anybody.

Bess: Maybe Mis' Fisher'd like to buy it.

Nick: I don't know. Wait a minute. (*Goes out door*) I'll show it to you.

Bess: Gee, that's too bad. Bought a bicycle and it's too small.

Vic: Yes, ma'm.

Nick: (*Coming back in*) It's a dandy bicycle too . . . coaster brake . . . siren horn . . . tool kit . . . saddle seat.

Vic: (*Gasps involuntarily*) Jiminy! It's a peach.

Nick: Don't know where I could sell it, do you, Vic?

Vic: How . . . how much is it?

Nick: Five cents. I paid more for it, but I've used it already so I guess I can't get such a fancy price. A nickel, take it.

Vic: I'll buy it. I got a nickel.

Nick: Where's the nickel? I'm not handing out anything on credit.

Vic: (*Eagerly*) Here, sir.

Nick: Wait a minute till I bite it. I'm not selling this for no phony nickel.

Vic: Is it all right?

Chapter Three 13

Nick: Yep. It's your bicycle.

Vic: Golly!

Bess: I'll run down and stir up the cakes. Call you when they're ready.

Nick: Alright, Bess. I'll show this fella how the bicycle works.

Vic: I know how it works, sir.

Nick: Aw, get out. Now look here, Vic, see these pedals?

Vic: Yes, sir.

Nick: They're to put your feet on.

Vic: (*Laughing*) I know that.

Nick: Just want to make sure is all. See these handlebars?

Vic: Yes, sir.

Nick: Ya put your hands on 'em . . . to guide with.

Vic: (*Laughing*) Uh-hum.

Nick: Now, don't get mixed up, will ya? Don't go putting your feet on the seat and your hands on the pedals.

Vic: (*Laughing*) No, sir. Freck Johnson can ride without any hands.

Nick: Get out!

Vic: Yes, he can. And with his eyes shut too.

Nick: Impossible!

Vic: I saw him.

Nick: Bet he peeked.

Vic: No, sir. He was riding downtown that way and he ran right into Mr. Peckinpaugh and tore his pants.

Nick: Whose pants?

Vic: Mr. Peckinpaugh's pants.

Nick: Mr. Peckinpaugh was riding the bicycle.

Vic: No, Freck Johnson was riding the bicycle.

Nick: And tore his pants.

Vic: No, he tore Mr. Peckinpaugh's pants.

Nick: That what I said. You were riding downtown with your eyes shut . . .

Vic: (*Laughing*) No, Freck Johnson was riding downtown . . .

Nick: I get ya, Steve.

Vic: Yes, sir.

Nick: Say, it's a funny thing, Vic. My name sounds awful close to yours.

Vic: Uh-huh.

Nick: Well, nobody's coming in here with a name that close to mine.

Vic: Yes, sir.

Nick: Is there anything else you'd like to be called besides Vic?

Vic: (*Eagerly*) Yes, call me Clay.

Nick: Clay?

Vic: Yes, that's my middle name. I like it.

Chapter Three

NICK: OKAY, CLAY. SAY, CLAY, WHAT DO YOU CALL . . . THE LADY?

VIC: THE NICE LADY DOWNSTAIRS?

NICK: YES, WHAT DO YOU CALL HER?

VIC: I CALL HER 'MA'M'

NICK: 'MA'M,' HUH? LISTEN, CLAY . . . WILL YA DO SOMETHING FOR ME?

VIC: (*EAGERLY*) OH, YES, SIR.

NICK: INSTEAD OF CALLING HER 'MA'M,' WILL YA CALL HER 'MOM'?

The show was "sustaining," which meant it had no sponsor; their salaries were paid by NBC. Gibby made $22.50 a week. Bert and Jeanette got $35 because they were adults. In spite of the fact that it came on the air at such an ungodly hour, they began getting fan mail, about twenty-five letters a day. After a while it started getting publicity, not much, but a small squib in the new radio magazines once in a while. It was clear that a small clique of listeners were out there enjoying the show. After broadcasting, Gibby was whisked to school, where he was reluctantly allowed the privilege of missing his first class by the school officials.

The show insinuated itself into his life. On Saturdays, instead of playing baseball or football, he often went to the racetrack with Wayne Tyler, the writer of *Nick and Bess*, with whom he had become friends. Wayne was in his late twenties, from Bloomington, Illinois, and was driving a cab in Chicago when he got hired by NBC because of a short story he'd written that got published in *Cosmopolitan*. His duties at the network consisted of writing lead-ins to musical numbers and jokes for comedy shows.

Wayne was a charming, offbeat guy who was known by his friends as the funniest guy in the world, and by some critics later on as the only genius to come out of radio. He loved people and wanted to make them laugh. He wrote letters and postcards constantly and sent them to everyone he knew. He also had a mischievous streak. He would write a highly obscene postcard to a secretary, generally a staid, unattractive one, and misdirect it to an address down the street. The shaken neighbor would appear at the secretary's home, gingerly holding the card. She professed not to have read it, but was merely returning it to its rightful owner.

Gibby would go down the hall at NBC to Wayne's cubbyhole in the writers' room and stand behind him as he wrote the show. He told Wayne that he noticed a lot of unfinished sentences and asked if the writer knew how they would end.

"No idea," said Wayne, continuing with his machine-gun typing.

For some reason Wayne found a compatible friend in Gibby, much to the younger man's delight. They went to the races, smoked cigars together and sometimes Wayne would let Gibby drive his old Cadillac. Being Wayne's friend gave Gibby a glow of confidence he'd never known before.

At the races, Wayne had a favorite stunt. A long shot would win, and Wayne would say, "Wait a minute . . . I think I've got a ticket on that horse . . ." And he would reach into his breast pocket and pull out the ticket. Then he would say, "Y'know, I think I've got another ticket on that horse . . ." And he would pull out a second ticket. He would continue the joke until he had a half-a-dozen tickets in his hand, and people around them would be gasping and laughing in shock. No one knew how many times he had the tickets when the horse lost, or how much money it cost him to pull off the joke, but that was Wayne.

The show was live, which meant it had to come out on time, on the dot. When it was a little long, they could cut some of the dialogue. If it was slightly short, the director signaled the actors to take their time by stretching his hands apart. But when it was really short Wayne would go down the hall to the nearest typewriter and type an insert that would fill a couple of minutes. Here's an insert:

BESS: HERE'S YOUR UNDERWEAR. HURRY UP AND GET INTO IT.

CLAY: MOM, HOW DO THEY MAKE UNDERWEAR?

BESS: HOW DO THEY MAKE IT?

CLAY: YEAH. HOW DO THEY . . . (*YAWNS*)

BESS: I DUNNO. I S'POSE THEY . . . I DON'T KNOW. MACHINE, I S'POSE.

CLAY: SEWIN' MACHINE?

BESS: I EXPECT. HERE, GIVE ME YOUR PAJAMAS.

CLAY: Here's the pants.

BESS: You're sittin' on the coat. Up.

CLAY: (*Chuckles*) Squirt was tellin' me how you can send away for underwear. He read it in a magazine. (*Laughs*) All ya hafta do is send 'em your size and they send you the underwear.

BESS: What's so funny about that?

CLAY: They had a real funny way of havin' ya send in your size. You're supposed to put some water in your bathtub, an' make a mark where the water come to an' then you get in the bathtub, an' make a mark where the water comes to then.

BESS: (*In disbelief*) No.

CLAY: (*Laughing*) Wait, I ain't through tellin' it. After ya got the two marks in the bathtub, ya put the bathtub in a crate or somethin' an send it to the underwear factory. An' they figure out your size an' send you the underwear.

BESS: (*Laughing*) Never heard anything so ridiculous.

CLAY: Funny thing, huh?

BESS: Squirt figure that out?

CLAY: No, he read it in a magazine. An' hey . . . (*Laughs*) if ya don't want to send in the bathtub, there's another way to get your size.

BESS: What's that?

CLAY: Well, ya fill the bathtub clean up to the top an' then you get in the bathtub, an' you catch the water that spills over, an' send that in. If you want loose fittin' underwear, all ya gotta do is add more water.

Nick and Bess went on for the next ten years. It got a sponsor, Procter and Gamble's Crisco, got a better time slot, paid the actors more money and achieved some fame. It was always one or two in the ratings for daytime shows. It was a satire on small-town life and attracted people with a wide range of interests. The ordinary housewife saw it as a comforting mirror of her own life, a little wacky sometimes, but warm and amusing. The slightly more sophisticated saw it as a subtle comedy that poked fun at the American small town. The intelligentsia saw it for what it was: A brilliantly wicked look at Americana, and the foibles of its freaky populace. Many famous people were hooked on it and made it a staple of their daily diet. It was rumored that on some film sets in Hollywood they halted shooting when the show came on and sat around to listen. Some celebrities came to the studio when they were in town and sat in the control room during the broadcast.

Gibby's mother and father separated during this time. They sold the house and his mother, Della, and Gibby moved to a two-bedroom apartment in the St. Clair Hotel on the north side of Chicago. It made more sense, since Gibby had to be in town every day, and there was little need for them to live with Ben in the suburbs.

Gibby was eleven when the show started and twenty when the Japanese bombed Pearl Harbor. He was in the lottery for the draft.

Chapter Four

Gibby was lying in the bathtub, letting the hot water trickle from the faucet onto his toes and listening to the little radio that stood on a chair next to the tub. He was thinking about suicide. Not actually determined to kill himself, but if it happened, he didn't give a shit. What was the life expectancy of a tail gunner in combat? Seven seconds? He reached over to the radio and, with a shaky hand, changed the station. When he told his psychiatrist about it several years later, he said he'd often heard stories about how people died fiddling with a radio while in the tub. "If it happened, it happened. If not . . ."

"You'd lay there and listen to the music," finished the doctor.

Bill Geller had called him into his office. "Listen, we've been talking to P. & G. and they want you protected from the draft. What's your number?"

"I don't know, but it's pretty high . . ."

"Well, they're nervous. I think you and I will go up tomorrow and get you enlisted."

"Yeah? And then what?"

"We'll get you situated somewhere safe, somewhere nearby, so you can keep doing the show."

"Jesus. Can you do that?"

"Are you kidding? We work for NBC. The Navy loves NBC. The Navy needs NBC."

"Yeah. But Jesus . . ."

"Don't worry about it. You wanna get your ass shot off? And there's a lot of money involved."

"I know, but . . ."

"We'll go up in the morning, when you're through with the show."

The next morning they drove up to the Great Lakes Naval Station in Geller's car. Gibby looked out the window as they moved up North Shore

Drive. The people who were crossing the road, running to the beach, were from another world now, he realized. The beach, the girls, the guys were not in the same hemisphere as him. No matter what happened, his life was changed from now on. He was going into the Navy. Jesus.

At the Naval Station, Gibby realized that Geller had prepared the ground. An officer, with gold on his sleeves and lapels, was expecting them. Not as many questions about what, as there were about where and when. Gibby hardly paid attention. But then, finally, he was taken to an office where he raised his right hand and was in the Navy.

"They didn't even give me a physical," he said as they were driving back.

"Don't worry about it. You won't be *doing* anything physical." Though he cringed at the prospect, he had to tell his mother. She was sitting near a window, crocheting. "Where you was?" she wanted to know.

"I drove up to the Naval Station, with Mr. Geller." She looked up, frowning, suspicion and fear in her eyes.

"Listen, Ma, I enlisted. I'm in the Navy."

"No! Gott in himmel! You're going away?"

"No. I'm going to be in the public relations department. A few blocks from here. They want me to keep doing the show."

She was not completely reassured. "You're not going in the war?"

"Well, not really . . . I'm going to be working in an office. And I'll be living here. There's no reason to worry . . ."

"But . . . But they could send you away . . ."

"No, I don't think so. They don't want to hurt the show. Procter and Gamble set it up. They want to keep me here. Probably for the duration."

He thought he ought to go out and see his father. Ben, now in his mid-seventies, spent his days at the Elk's Club in Oak Park. He was proud of the fact that he was only one of three Jews who had been accepted into the club. He'd rented out the tavern and lived mostly on the income.

Now they sat side by side in easychairs in the lounge of the club. They'd never had much to talk about. But now, apparently, Ben thought he ought to say something, given the circumstances. "So you're in the Navy, huh?"

"Right."

"But yer gonna be livin' with Ma at the hotel."

"Yeah."

"Ya don't think you'll get in the war?"

"I don't know. NBC set it up. The sponsor wants me to keep doing the show."

"I see. Well, yer better off. You could get killed. Or lose an arm, or a leg."

"I suppose."

"Ma's probably happy that yer gonna stay out of it."

"Uh-huh."

"She'd probably kill herself if anything happened to you."

Chapter Five

Navy Public Relations was in the 333 building at Michigan Boulevard and Wacker Drive, about three blocks from the hotel. It was an office with a lot of guys in sailor suits running around. They welcomed him dispassionately. The guys were O.K., former newspaper guys and a few from advertising agencies who had low draft numbers. They seemed determined to pretend they were in the real Navy, saying things like, "At seventeen—forty-five we've got to . . ." And, "You want a cup of Joe?" A guy with a bland, round face and white hair, Oliver, said that, and then added, "That's what they call it in the Navy."

When he appeared at the studio in his uniform, they were, for the most part, amused and made a lot of gory jokes. Jeanette asked Wayne if he was going to enlist. He replied in the negative.

"Have you ever shot a gun?" she asked.

"No, the first thing I'll shoot will be the Japanese."

Working at the Public Relations office was not pleasant. He had no right to be there. His job was a sham, and everyone knew it. His fellow workers knew he was only hiding out from the hostilities and showed their contempt. He was given the most odious duties, like watches on Christmas and New Year's Eve, where he had to mind the switchboard all night long. They didn't hate him, but didn't mind punishing him just the same. And he was constantly full of guilt; he was sure people at the studio and at the hotel secretly made fun of his wearing the uniform. He applied for a transfer to the Navy Air Corps.

The director of **Nick and Bess** was a tall, skinny, acerbic fellow. "I'll bet your friends at the office hate your guts living at home and doing the show," he said.

"No, I think they like me," said Gibby, but he wasn't all that sure.

Meanwhile, months passed and he heard nothing about his application for the air corps. Several times, he drove up to the Naval Station to see Jackie Beavers, head of the transfers department. Then one day, Eric, one of his fellow workers, announced that he had received orders to pre-flight training. Gibby was on him like a flash.

"When did you apply?" he wanted to know.

"About three weeks ago."

"How did you get it so quick? I've been waiting forever."

"I took flying lessons and got a solo license, and sent it in with my application."

Gibby was stunned. What a simple thing to do! How stupid he'd been! The next Saturday Gibby was at the airport in Northridge. Six weeks later, in a snowstorm, he soloed. He fired the solo license in to Miss Beavers, and in another week or so, had his orders. He was to go to pre-flight in ten days.

This was when he changed the radio station in the bathtub. He lied to his mother, telling her that he was being sent to San Francisco to help open a new office. He went in to Geller and told him the bad news. Geller was philosophical. "I figured you'd do something stupid like that, eventually." He informed the cast and Wayne, all of whom were sympathetic and supportive.

There was a certain satisfaction in telling his father, even though it was hard to ascertain exactly what the old man's real feelings were.

"You're givin' up a good salary . . ."

"Yeah."

"What're you makin' now?"

"Four-fifty a week."

"That's a lot of money."

"I know it. The main thing, though, is not to let Ma find out."

"I won't say anything."

Ben never quite understood Gibby's being on the radio. He always worried that the boy would never get a real job.

"I was in Cuba when I was in the war."

"Yeah. Spanish-American war, right?"

"Right. I was too short to get in. But I stood on my toes."

"I remember you telling me that. What did you do when you were in Cuba?"

"I rode a mule into town every day and picked up the mail."

"Huh."

"My ass was sore all the time."

Gibby laughed.

"Well, listen, I'm sure you got a lot to do . . ."

The conversation was over. They stood up and hugged. A small sound escaped from his father's throat. "Be careful."

"I'll try. So long, Dad . . ." Ben remained standing, watching his son all the way to the door, where Gibby turned and waved. "I'll see you . . ."

Chapter Six

There were two more people he had to say goodbye to: Mary and Viola Wilson. Viola, a widow, managed the tennis courts on Huron Street, where Gibby played tennis in the afternoons. She had two kid; Jim, nineteen, a blond Adonis, possessor of a prodigious cock, according to his mother. His younger sister, Mary, was a tightly packed blonde who sat in shorts on a ledge in front of the booth when Gibby played, with her knees up and her arms around her knees inviting his visualization of the ultimate prize.

One afternoon Viola invited Gibby up to their flat in the building next to the courts. Viola, Mary and Gibby had a few drinks and the mother told Gibby about the Greek gentleman who lived on the floor below. "He's ugly as sin, but he brings us lamb chops, and stuffed grape leaves and all kinds of Greek food. He's got the idea he can get into my pants and I string him along. It's great food."

The three of them began going out on Friday nights, starting with the clubs on Rush Street. Viola and Mary liked to drink, and they could put away a lot. But usually their booze was paid for by guys who were trying to pick them up. Viola used Mary as bait. Men were instantly attracted to Mary's fresh, tempting appearance, but were soon sidetracked by her mother's gregarious, more promising manner. Viola was also Mary's tutor in the ways of men. "You don't have to do anything," she told her daughter. "Just tell 'em how good it is."

They would then proceed to the after-hours joints that opened after the regular clubs closed, where the strippers and prostitutes went for a drink. It was an education for Gibby. He learned that most strippers had a seven-year-old son who was being cared for by her mother, and the same for the hookers. But they were fun to talk to, and Viola and Mary knew a lot of them.

When Gibby drove them home, Viola, sometimes with a guy she'd picked up, would go upstairs. Gibby and Mary would remain in the car and do some heavy petting. But not go all the way. He'd been brainwashed by his sister and mother that it would be disaster if he got anyone pregnant. Also, he realized later, in therapy, he was pretty frightened of intimacy.

They were driving in his car. Viola was in the front seat with her latest boyfriend, a cop. He and Mary were in the back. They were driving south along the beach on a velvety summer night. A full moon. Viola and the cop were laughing hysterically.

"Six!" he yelled out.

"No!"

"Absolutely! Six!"

"God! I only came four. Six to four. That's a set!"

The cop pulled a sudden U-turn. He knew a secret road down to the beach. They bumped over a sandy trail that was nothing more than two tire tracks. After a bit, near the water, he stopped. "Nobody comes here. Nobody knows about it."

They got out and looked at the water. Viola had the idea. "Let's all take our clothes off and go swimming!" They did so, and ran to the water like a bunch of kids. God, how great it felt! Gibby had never felt so free and abandoned. To be naked and playing in the water, with the cars zooming by, and the city all around them, and no one knowing they were there! It was like being alone in the Garden of Eden. They splashed each other and yelled at each other and dove between each other's legs. Gibby, finally exhausted, was the first to make his way back to the sand. He went up a little ways and sat down. Viola and the cop had disappeared. He saw only Mary swimming offshore.

She waded slowly to the beach and then emerged. He gasped. The moon lit her hair from behind and her body, coming out of the surf. Botticelli! She came slowly up to him and sat down almost touching him. It was difficult for him to speak, but he finally burbled, "God, you're beautiful!"

"So are you."

"Bullshit."

He put his arms around her. They felt each other all over. He had never been so aroused. His hands slid over her wet skin, her legs, her breast, until finally, he came in the sand.

Now he was climbing the stairs to their apartment. He heard music, and knocked on the door. "Come in," yelled Viola from inside. He opened the door and found the two of them dancing to the music from a record player and drinking vodka. They were delighted to see him and Viola poured him a drink.

Several drinks later, after he told them he was going away, Gibby fell back on the bed. The room was spinning slowly around him. He felt something happening at his fly and raised his head to see Viola, smiling, unbuttoning his pants. With Mary looking on, her mother bent forward, and said goodbye in a way he would never forget.

Chapter Seven

St. Mary's College was set among trees in the rolling countryside of Moraga, California, the wine country, a serene posh school just north of San Francisco. It was taken over by the Navy as a pre-flight school whose students were housed in Quonset huts instead of dormitories. After a crowded, sweltering train ride from Chicago about two dozen fledgling pilots were put on a bus and driven to the school. They were shaken to see, as they entered the campus, a number of young men with casts on their arms and legs, and many using crutches. All of these disabled men waved at the bus when they saw it, and yelled: "Go back! Go back!" Gibby and his new friends smiled weakly at each other.

But they found out they had been well advised. St. Mary's was a place to test the soul and body. It was initiation time. The faculty, mostly professional athletes, were there to see how tough the newcomers were. And if they were not tough enough, they were made tough or washed out. You did everything until you dropped, even basketball. If you ran, you ran until you fell, unable to move. If you swam, you swam until you floundered in the water and had to be pulled out with a pole. The first night, at dinner, someone came up behind Gibby and put his hand on Gibby's shoulder. It was Eric. Gibby reached back and grabbed Eric above the knee. It felt like grabbing iron. "My God, you've been exercising," said Gibby. "You have no idea," said Eric. "But you'll find out."

They were told to pick a main sport. Gibby picked boxing. He wanted to do it the hard way, to prove something, and Ben had taught him a little. The boxers met on the lawn the first afternoon, in two lines, facing each other, all wearing boxing gloves. One from each line stepped up in turn and faced their opponent from the other line. Then they sparred for a few minutes. The guy who came forward to meet Gibby was thick and tough looking. Gibby tilted his head to the left and threw an overhand right which landed flush on the other guy's jaw, dropping him to the ground.

"O.K.," said the instructor.

The instructor, who was a former basketball player of some renown, didn't like him. Maybe he wasn't enough of a jock. He wasn't as fit as most of the others, having spent most of his young life in a radio studio, or maybe he just wasn't the instructor's kind of guy, or maybe the instructor suspected him of being Jewish. They were divided into teams of eight and sparred among themselves every afternoon, and then ran four miles around the lake. Once a week they each had an inter-team fight in the ring with a referee and corner men and the whole nine yards. When Gibby stepped into the ring for his first fight, his corner man said, "I heard this guy is not very good."

Gibby said, "Well, I'm not either, so we're even."

But surprisingly, Gibby won the fight. The instructor looked at him with, perhaps, more respect, but little more affection. A week later, he won another fight. His instructor regarded him with narrowed eyes.

Jarvis, a young man on his team, was said to have had a lot of amateur fights and figured to turn pro when the war interrupted his plans. Don, the instructor, put a hand on Gibby's shoulder. "I want you and Jarvis to spar today."

The rest of the team sort of drifted into a circle, watching, as Gibby and Jarvis approached each other, putting up their hands. For Gibby, it was like being in a hailstorm. A hailstorm of gloves. The punches came so fast and from so many directions, he couldn't even fight back. He staggered in reverse just trying to cover up. But then, suddenly, Jarvis stopped and stepped back. Gibby lowered his gloves and peered at his opponent. He couldn't quite read what was in the other man's face. Maybe a feeling that he'd hit his adversary enough. Or maybe he was just weary and taking a small rest. In any case, the frustration in Gibby erupted in a fury. He sprang forward and threw a windmill of punches, some of them landing.

"O.K., that's enough," said Don.

One of his teammates walked with Gibby back to the Quonset hut. "You did pretty good," he said.

"Hell," said Gibby, "he just got tired beating on me."

But the next morning Jarvis woke up with a black eye, the result of one of Gibby's desperate blows, and he was an instant celebrity, known as "the guy who gave Jarvis a black eye."

He was approached by another fellow in their hut. "Listen, you used to be on a radio show, weren't you? My mother used to listen to it every day. I heard it myself a couple of times when I was home sick from school."

"Jesus, don't tell anybody, will you? I don't want any of these other guys to know . . ."

"Why not?"

"I don't know. I'd just feel funny about it."

"O.K." Gibby and this fellow, known as "Stub," got to be friends, probably through sharing the secret.

There was a lot of rain. It was February, the midst of the rainy season, and it rained twenty-six out of the twenty-eight days. They hiked in the rain and mud—Moraga mud, they called it, and it was like glue. The hikes included a lot of double-time and running, and they went for miles. A lot of guys dropped from exhaustion, especially after getting shots.

There were also the "rainy-day programs" when they went to the gym and had the "Fight for Life." After a few setting-up exercises the mats were brought out and the cadets were divided into pairs.

"Anything goes," said the jock instructor. "You can hit a man with your fist; you can kick him in the balls. There's only one thing you can't do. You can't claw his eyes. You'll need those for later on." The instructors supervised the fights, to make sure nobody went blind. But the struggles continued until one man was unconscious. The way it usually happened was that one guy completely ran out of strength. Then his opponent choked him. The instructor was also there to see there were no fatalities.

Gibby got a letter from Wayne.

Mother Theresa,

Speaking of rumble seats here's a funny joke. You say to some poor dupe, "What is the difference between a rumble seat and a boar's cock?" "I give up," he'll rejoin. "They're both comfortable in a pig's ass!" is your topper.

And another; two elderly gents were dabbling their toes in the Atlantic at Miami Beach. One said, "Permit me to introduce myself; I'm Mister Spalding." "To be sure," exclaimed the other, "I've often played with your balls. Now let me introduce myself. I'm Mister Planters." "Mr. Planters, dear fellow, I couldn't begin to tell you how many times I've chewed your nuts!"

This is National Tavern Month. Just think; mother rates only one day, the saloon thirty.

Many unique colorful shrines have been built on the Church grounds at Dickeyville, Wis., a village of 258 people. Pebbles, stones, shells and corals from all parts of the world were collected by a priest and built into these beautiful monuments dedicated to religion and patriotism.

Dear William:
    At this most significant time of the year I'm sure our hearts turn trustfully towards the glorious tenets so beautifully laid down for us in the tender mercies and sweet remembrances without which the gift of life never fails to hearken and to rejoice.

    P.S. I still have the clap.

Chapter Eight

Pre-flight dragged on and bodies got harder. After eight weeks, they had liberty and Gibby hoped somebody might challenge him on the streets of San Francisco.

They were all called into a room and an officer addressed them. He said if any of them wanted to go into the "Lighter than Air" service, they could get their commissions at once and begin duty, avoiding the rest of pre-flight and later flight training. There were a few volunteers but not many, although it was tempting to think of becoming an officer immediately, and skip the trials that lay ahead.

They were approaching transfer to the next level: Primary Flight Training. They made out the first of many wills, designating next of kin and the recipients of their worldly goods. They were also asked what sort of service they preferred: Fighters, Bombers, or Torpedo planes. Gibby chose Fighters, because he figured that to be the most dangerous. There were two installations they could be sent to: Long Beach, California, or some place in Iowa. The word was to pray for Long Beach, since the other was a dreary place with few opportunities to get laid.

Gibby was delighted to learn he had drawn Long Beach, along with "Stub."

Long Beach was great, surrounded by orange groves and within hitchhiking distance of Hollywood. The plane they would be flying was the venerable Stearman, a yellow biplane that had been the training vehicle for thousands of military pilots. It was said of the Stearman that if you got in trouble, the best solution was to take your hands and feet off the controls and it would fly itself. Gibby and his friends found that to be something of an overstatement. His instructor was Ted Combs, a skinny, tall red-haired guy of about thirty who had survived the sinking of the *Hornet* by Japanese torpedo planes. His nerves were still fragile. If you dropped a penny behind him, he would jump six feet. But he was a cheery fellow and tolerant. And he seemed to like Gibby.

His main problem was landings. The Stearman's wheels were close together and the lower wing was only about two feet off the ground so that the tiniest gust of wind caused a ground loop, where the wing tip touched the earth and the plane spun like a top. He was put on a ground-loop trainer, where he sat on a wooden seat, delicately balanced, and had to correct immediately when it leaned to one side or the other. But then he was transferred to morning flights when the wind was milder and his troubles with landings were over.

Ted sat in the front seat and communicated with his student in the rear by one-way phone. The student was unable to reply. They started with touch-and-go landings, where they circled the field, landed, and before coming to a stop, hit the throttle and took off again. After dialing in on this exercise, they went on to a regular list of maneuvers that they repeated every day. They flew figure eights around two pylons, where the pilot had to gauge the wind so that the "eights" were not lopsided. They flew around an outlying field until the instructor abruptly cut the throttle and let the student figure how to make a safe emergency landing. This usually required sideslipping into the field.

Finally, they went on to Aerobatics, the downfall of so many student pilots. There were loops, Immelmans, snap-rolls and slow-rolls, spins and falling leaves. This was to prepare them for dogfighting, although Ted said that in combat the most effective move was a tight turn.

The slow-roll was the bugaboo for most of the young pilots since it was rather complicated, requiring the reversal of controls several times during the maneuver. For instance, in a slow-roll to the left, you began with moving the stick to the left and back a bit, to keep the nose up and the plane revolving counterclockwise. At this point, the rudder began to act as the elevator and the elevator as the rudder. At the same time, the right pedal was depressed to help keep the nose up. When the plane was upside-down, the stick was moved forward and brought to the center. The left pedal was depressed to keep the revolution going. When the plane was on its right side, the stick was moved to the left and rearward to keep the nose up and the plane going counterclockwise. The series of movements of the controls was necessary to keep the plane revolving slowly on a straight and level axis.

Gibby was obsessed by the need to accomplish this feat. He certainly was not going to get washed out by not being able to do a slow-roll. So he practiced the sequence of operations again and again, using an imaginary stick, and moving his feet as if they were on the pedals.

When Gibby first demonstrated the slow-roll to Ted, he could hear the instructor chuckling to himself on the phone. Of course, he was following the movements of the controls in his cockpit. When they were right-side-up again, he said, "Not bad." Then he took over the controls and swooped down to land next to an orange grove. They got out and picked oranges and ate them on the ground next to the plane. Ted was so proud of his student he asked a fellow instructor to go up with Gibby so the young pilot could show his wares.

His skill at aerobatics was actually a surprise to Gibby because he'd expected to have a hard time with them. However, there was still a trial ahead. He was due for his first check-ride, which meant he had to fly a test flight with another instructor and successfully demonstrate all the maneuvers he'd learned in order to be allowed to go to the next level. To fail at any of them meant a down-check. Two down-checks and you were washed out.

His own weakness was emergency landings. He needed practice, but there was a huge obstacle. Emergency landings could only be carried out with an instructor in the plane. To ignore that rule was a serious infraction. Gibby weighed the downside and decided to take the chance. They were now being allowed a certain number of solo flights, and on his next one he went directly to the outlying field. He spent the next two hours flying around it, cutting the gun at every possible position and twisting down to a landing. However, just as he was about to head back, he saw another yellow plane begin to circle the field, and he could only hope that the instructor flying it didn't see that he was alone.

Bad luck. He had been observed and reported. Notified to see the Chief Flight Officer immediately, he made his way over to the Ad building on shaky legs. Officer Bradley had him come into his office. "I guess you know why you're here," he said.

"Yes, sir."

"What's your explanation?"

There was no excuse. At least not a reasonable one. Gibby stood there, unable to speak, and then suddenly he was spouting words, hardly aware of what he was saying. "I don't want to wash out! I want those wings! I'd do anything . . . I knew it was wrong, but compared to washing out . . . I took a chance! Do you understand?"

The grey-haired Bradley stared at him impassively for a long moment. Then he reached up and touched his own wings. "Yeah," he said. "I do. Dismissed."

Dear Dungheap.

I'll start off with a god dam funny joke. A man with standing (should be 'was') in a stall in the men's can at the Union Station. The guy next to him was black as your shoe. But our hero noticed that the black man's cock was white as your shirt. He said, "It's none of my business, friend, and perhaps I'm intrusive but I'm in show business and I can make your fortune for you." The black man replied, "I'm not interested but I'm grateful for your interest. It happnes that I'm a professional chimney sweep. I'm on my honeymoon."

No, but when you wrote and asked me what I thought of Florsheim shoes as a product, I think I can be truthful in saying that they give superlative wear, are comfortable on the feet, maintain their neat appearance, and give a man a good robust value for his money. For some years I wore Florsheims exclusively and feel no restraint in averring that I received perfect satisfaction. A neighbor of mine - Mike Spranze - prefers French, Shriner and Urner shoes. My wife's father has been a lifetime wearer of the Nettleton last. But I give Florsheims my unqualified approval. You can have that opinion for what it's worth.

Well, Gibby I know you're a busy man and I won't take up any more of your time. I think I have pretty well sized up the situation and if there are any points in this letter you find confusing just drop me a line. You can readh me in care of the Western Avenue street car barns here in Chicago where I have been helping out in the evenings.

And don't worry too much about the money. Take all the time in the world. However, if you feel like sending thirty or forty dollars just to show good faith, why, <u>fine</u>.

Now - until next Sunday evening at this same hour, Swift and Company, and your announcer - Jean Paul King - wish you a pleasant weekend and - good night.

Your affectionate mother

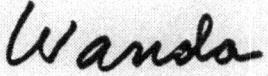

Chapter Nine

The last two weeks of their time at Long Beach, they were introduced to a new airplane—the Tim. This plane, in contrast to the stubby, old-fashioned design of the Stearman, was a sleek, low-winged monoplane that really looked hot. Gibby loved it, loved flying it. They went into formation flying now, learning to keep a wing within a few inches of another wing, no matter where that wing went or what it did. If it went into a loop, you went into a loop. If it dived, you dived. The wing you were flying on was your magnet and kept your full attention until you peeled off for a landing.

From now on, formation flying was part of their lives, and eventually they were able to fly together, perhaps a few inches apart, as if they were one plane.

Advanced training. The final hurdle before getting their wings! Again, there were two places they could be sent to—Pensacola, in the panhandle of Florida, and Corpus Christi in Texas. According to the scuttlebutt there was little to choose between them. Pensacola, in the poorest section of Florida, was a dismal place with no social attractions. Corpus might be even worse. It was practically on the border of Mexico and was as hot as Hades most of the year.

Gibby got Corpus. They would be flying SNJs, the Navy's most advanced trainer. It had guns and was equipped for instrument flying. Corpus was divided into a number of fields, each specializing in one phase of training. One was for gunnery, one for dive-bombing, etc.

The place was hot, beastly hot. It was August, and a fresh shirt lasted about ten minutes before it was completely soaked through. The only relief, in a rare moment of leisure, was to take off all your clothes, lay flat on the bed with the windows open and pray for a breeze.

The students were divided into four-man teams. In gunnery, one man pulled the target, a ten-foot cylinder made of canvas, while the instructor and the other three students made runs on it. Each student had bullets with a different color on the tip. After the session they would surround the target, which lay on the ground, and tote up their score. But getting the target into the air was a tough assignment. A hundred-foot rope was attached to the plane with the target on the other end. A crewman laid out the rope on the left side of the runway, ahead of the plane. The pilot of the target plane revved his engine to the max and then burst into his takeoff. When he got almost to the target, he pulled back the stick and went into as steep a climb as possible without stalling. When the maneuver was successful, the canvas cylinder was pulled straight up off the ground and into the air. If the pilot miscalculated or got timid, the canvas was pulled along the runway and became a tattered mess.

The target plane headed out over the ocean. The other planes flew to the side and slightly above the target in a straight line. When they were in position the instructor waggled his wings and went into his run. His run demonstrated the sort of run he wanted from the others. It could be from the side, from directly above or an opposite end run from beneath. The opposite end run was a bit hairy. The shooting planes pulled ahead and on a level with the target plane. One by one, they peeled off and flew directly head-on at the target plane; when they got close, they dived under the target plane and pulled up shooting at the target as it was pulled over their heads.

There were mock dogfights and dive-bombing runs. The instructor occasionally played follow-the-leader with them. They were in a line, behind the instructor. He did a maneuver and each plane in turn did the same, all the way down the line.

The most interesting and difficult activity was instrument flying. They started in Link trainers, a mock-up of a cockpit. In front of them was a schematic sketch of a radio station that would guide them to a landing field. The station sent out signals in the pattern of a cross. By flying a certain pattern they determined which leg of the cross they encountered. Then they followed the leg to see if the volume of the signal increased or diminished, indicating whether they were approaching or getting farther away from the station. Once they were oriented on the signal, they followed it to the field.

It may sound simple but the budding pilots had all kinds of trouble solving the problem. As the students flew the Link trainer, their path was traced and printed on a machine outside the room. Gibby was shown a diagram of his flight pattern, and the woman in charge of the machine said they were putting it on the board as an example of how it should be done. His pride knew no bounds.

After ten hours or so in the Link trainer, they tried it in the air. Now the student occupied the front cockpit and the instructor the rear. The student was covered by a canopy, which completely obscured the outside. The instructor flew to an unknown destination and turned over the controls to the student. Now the student, who could see only the instruments and hear the radio signals, had to find his way to the field.

After the lengthy exposure to the process in the Link, it was not too difficult. Gibby methodically eliminated the false moves and found the correct ones. Then, with the signals getting louder and louder, the instructor popped the canopy and Gibby found he was directly over the goal.

Instrument training was conducted at one of the subsidiary installations at Beeville. Beeville was a quaint town that was somewhat of a surprise to a lad from Chicago. The men on the street carried guns on their hip, like in a Western movie. Anyone who wondered why was told it was a protection against snakes.

Gibby, on liberty in Beeville, went to a hotel and discovered a really effective relief from the heat. There was no such thing as air conditioning, but he found that if he removed his clothes and lay on the bed under the fan, it was possible to spend a few bearable hours. It was also in this hotel that he lost his virginity, formally. The elevator operator, a black gentleman of about three hundred pounds, asked him casually if he'd like some company this evening. Gibby said, sure, then waited nervously in his room.

After a while, there was a knock on his door, and he called out to come in. A slender blonde girl, about eighteen, bounced in. She pulled at the zipper that ran down the front of her dress, shrugged out of it and was nude, except for her shoes, which she kicked off. She dropped onto the bed and held out her hand. "Twenty bucks," she said. Gibby took out his wallet and paid her.

"O.K., Sailor," she said, "come and get it."

Gibby lay down beside her and put his arm around her. After a time, she said, "Hey, are you a virgin?"

"Well, kind of . . ."

"What does that mean?"

"Well, I had an experience once . . ."

"Yeah?"
"Yeah. My girlfriend's mother . . ."
"What!"
"Went down on me."
"You're kidding."
"No."
"Where was your girlfriend?"
"Right there. Watching."
The hooker began to laugh. "Shit! I never heard anything like that!"
"Really?"
"Uh-uh. You're a swinger."
"Thanks."
"Well, come on. You'll get the hang of it."

Gibby did. But after she left, he was in a panic. He'd seen so many clap movies. He ran down the street to where he'd seen the sign: Emergency Clinic, and confessed to the orderly that he'd just had a sexual encounter. The orderly asked if he'd used a condom, and Gibby said, yes, the hooker had provided one.

"Then what are you worried about?"
"I don't know. I wanted to be sure."

He got a shot, just in case, and felt better.

Dear old pal:

You haven't heard from me because I was visited by another attack of influenza (or its little brother). Chicago has had its worst winter in all history and that's been tough on frail flowers of advanced years like myself. However, I feel today that I may recover. This latest bout with illness has been highlighted by a reactivation of my norally, should be normally, dormant hemorrhoids. Massive dose of something called, I believe, Stereomycin occasioned astonishingly frequent bathroom summonses which threw my posterior machinery into a state of imbalance. My piles are the itching variety and when I venture out on the street I'm apt to walk more and more rapidly until I'm travelling at a dead run. Also I have a tendency to jump over fire hydrants and yelp little nervous yelps. The snapshot above supplies a notion of how a person feels when his hemorrhoids are itching.

Although we won't be able to make the scene on Christmas Eve our hearts are with you and we extend heartiest best wishes for another robust and prosperous half century.

I am enclosing a birthday card. It pictures Miss Beulah Fisher and me. We are currently living together at the Sweet Surrender Cut-rate Motel in Pullman, Illinois. Miss Fisher plays request piano numbers at the F. W. Woolworth Ten Cent Store at 125th Street and Agatite Avenue here in Chicago. Her take-home pay (with tips) often exceeds $65.00 per week. It is our only income. You may be surprised at the costume I'm wearing in the photograph. As a matter of fact I am now a free-lance clergyman. Two other guys and myself founded the Des Moines Believers in the Radiant Future. For $3.75 I will preach you a sermon. For $4.00 even Miss Fisher and I will follow the sermon with a vocal duet: "It Was Only a Paper Moon."

Little joke:

    CONWAY TEARLE: What has eleven yellow ass holes and wings?

    DOROTHY MACKAIL: I give up.

    CONWAY TEARLE: A Chinese football team.

        HAPPY BIRTHDAY!

Wayne

Chapter Ten

Back on the main base, he was on a gunnery run when his engine began spraying oil all over his windshield. He could barely see. He radioed the instructor and told him about the problem, and was told to return to the base. Gibby flew to the shore but couldn't recognize any landmarks. Aimlessly, he flew inland and tried to find the field. He flew in circles, without a clue. Then he saw railroad tracks below and decided to follow them north, figuring he would run into some place where he could land. About twenty minutes later he spied an airfield, not his own, but better than nothing. He didn't know which base it was, so he couldn't radio them for landing instructions.

He looked for a windsock, so he could at least land in the right direction, saw one and then discovered a runway that seemed to go upwind. He flew once around the field, and, finding it clear, went in for a landing.

Taxiing back to the buildings, he was picked up by a flag man and directed to a stall. He went inside the main building and entered the first office he came to. He told his troubles to the officer sitting at a desk. The officer shook his head. "You went in exactly the wrong direction. If you'd gone south, you would have run into the base."

"I couldn't really see," said Gibby. "Could you spare some gas? I'm almost out."

Windshield cleaned, gas in the tank, he took off and headed home. Thirty minutes after landing, he was standing before the Officer of the Day. That gentleman was perusing a paper before him. "Let's see . . . you got lost, found the wrong field, landed on the wrong runway, took off on the wrong runway, and cut an instructor out of the flight pattern when you landed here. Did you do anything right?"

"Well, I brought the plane back, sir."

"Congratulations. Thirty demerits." Each demerit meant an hour marching alone, with a gun on his shoulder, around the mess hall while everyone else had dinner.

Another officer from Washington appeared before the cadets. "As you may, or may not know, Marine pilots get the same training as Navy pilots. They are being trained right alongside you now. We have openings for a few of you who would like to switch to the Marines. If so, you will graduate at the same time, but be land-based, and never take off or land on a carrier." Although this last was said in the most casual of tones, they all knew what he was getting at, since many cadets had anxiety about flying off a carrier. Gibby and most of his friends ignored the offer, but there were a number of others, who leapt at the chance to avoid the perils of carrier operation.

Graduation was fast approaching. Soon they would have their wings and commissions. They got time off to be measured for officer's uniforms amid high excitement. During the year of training, most of them believed this moment would never arrive. They were almost hysterical when the uniforms were delivered. They had epaulets with a single stripe, and were to be addressed as Ensign in barely a week.

The day of graduation was dour, with a few snowflakes in the air. Della was among the onlookers. An officer, followed by an enlisted man, walked along the line, carrying a small box. The enlisted man called out the cadet's name and the officer took a pair of wings from the box and pinned it on the man's breast. Della was wiping her eyes when Gibby got his.

He and his sister went to dinner at a place that had only one entrée: chicken-fried steak. But what the hell, there was a war on.

"How's Ma doing?" he wanted to know.

"Well, she knows . . ."

"That I'm in the air corps?"

"Yeah. We figured we had to tell her . . . You could be gone a long time."

"And how did she take it?"

"Well, she drank the whole bottle of her red medicine."

"No! My God! What happened?"

"Nothing. I talked to the doctor, and he said it was just sugar water."

"Are you kidding! Her red medicine? All these years . . ."

"She held that red medicine over our heads . . ."

"Yeah! Every time we did anything, or wanted to do something she didn't like . . ."

"She said she'd take the whole bottle of red medicine and kill herself." They laughed until other patrons turned and looked at them as if they were nuts.

Thursday

Sweetest Gibby:

I'm glad your pop is comfortably circumstanced.

Frank Walsh and I went to the Washington Park race track the other Saturday and lost our god dam ass.

I am driving to Bloomington, Illinois, on Saturday and interview a prospective tenant for my house. I expect to spend the night in Lincoln, Illinois, with the Partlows. Partlow is still wheeling and dealing. He's selling those fancy Chevy Impala convertibles as fast as they're delivered.

Roy Winsor visited a few weeks ago. His father died. Roy's business is strong and prosperous.

Bill Koblenzer phoned the other evening.

Mary Fran's pop (widowed a year ago) spent the winter in Florida and is just back. He is 74 and full of piss.

I play chess every Monday night with Jack Dunn. He used to be a continuity writer at NBC. We have played 89 games and Jack is 9 ahead.

Let's see: you must be within a cunt hair of *23*. Jesus Christ Almighty!

Will close..........

Wayne

Chapter Eleven

He had orders to Melbourne, Florida, for operational training, which meant he was now going to fly real Honest-to-God fighter planes. "Stub" was going there too, and some of his other friends. They were all scared. The first time they flew the Grumman, they would be all alone. There was only one seat in the damn thing! The thought of that first flight made their testicles tighten up. They would also be shooting six fifty-caliber guns and dropping real bombs. This was it, baby!

Melbourne was a lovely place. It was like being on a winter vacation. The beach was right outside. Flowers bloomed everywhere. At the entrance to their Quonset hut there was a tree bearing large, ripe grapefruit. But still they had to fly that six-hundred-mile-an-hour beast alone the first time!

They started with pictures of the inside of the cockpit: the myriad of instruments, controls and gauges. They were told to memorize the layout. Then they sat in a mock-up of the cockpit, one by one, with an instructor standing at their elbow. He would call out the names of various instruments, etc. and they had to reach out and touch them immediately. Then they were blindfolded, and asked to do the same. Any hesitation drew a reprimand and an order to study harder.

They went out to the flight line and looked at the dark blue Hellcats. God, they were big! They had all had the impression that fighter planes were small and nimble, but this baby was big and heavy. Somebody on the flight line said seven tons. That's a lot of iron when you're trying to evade a Zero, or landing on a carrier deck. Part of the weight was a four-inch lead plate behind the pilot to protect him from enemy bullets.

The day arrived. They were going to take their first flight in the Hellcat. Nobody had slept much; they smiled sheepishly at each other as they got into their flight suits. The instructor was at the blackboard, showing them where the field was that they were going to. "It's a small field, about ten miles from here. You'll follow me over. Circle it once then one at a time, you'll peel off and land. I want five touch-and-go landings a piece and then go home."

They walked to the flight line. The eight planes were waiting in a row.

The enlisted men who stood in front of them seemed to be wearing an invisible smile. But they helped the new officers mount the planes for the first time. "Put your right foot in here, sir. Swing your left onto the wing. Now step into the cockpit. Very good, sir. Now buckle up."

Gibby sat there, buckled, sitting on his parachute, staring at the instruments, feeling a strong desire to get out and run. What was he doing there? He felt completely incompetent to fly this monster. The crewman was making circles with his right hand signaling him to start the engine, and Gibby, without thought, did so. The roar was deafening, unexpected. Two thousand horses! It was hard to breathe. Then the plane on his right was moving out, beckoned by the crewman with two wands, and Gibby pressed gently on the throttle. He was moving! He touched the right brake and the plane spun slowly to the right and he was following the plane ahead of him. Too late to back out now. He was part of the parade. It was survive or perish. Automatically he followed the plane ahead of him to the takeoff point and waited while the planes ahead, one by one, accelerated down the runway.

Now it was his turn. When the plane ahead of him was halfway down the runway, he moved forward onto the strip. When the other plane lifted into the air, Gibby made his mind a blank and opened the throttle all the way. His head snapped back against the headrest. Never had he felt such acceleration! He wasn't breathing. When the plane began feeling light he pulled back on the stick, and he was flying the Goddamn F-6-F!

In the air, he relaxed slightly. The plane was heavy, ten times more powerful than anything he'd flown before, but responsive. His previous training kicked in, and a feeling of familiarity took over. It was just an airplane after all, and he had learned to fly a plane, hadn't he? The group had merged into a loose formation and they were following the leader to the practice field.

He looked down and received a shock. There was the field just ahead, with a line of ambulances parked along the strip and guys in white clothes standing around. There were also several emergency trucks.

They circled the field. Gibby could see the paramedics looking up at them. The instructor was going in for his landing, and the rest of the flight was spreading out to give each guy some space. Finally, it was Gibby's turn. He banked to his left and cut back on the throttle. He was startled at how quickly the plane dropped. It was so heavy. He could see that any decrease in power meant an immediate loss of altitude.

Regaining control, he watched the earth speed toward him, easing the throttle and raising the nose to reduce the rate of descent. After an eternity he felt the wheels touch the ground and an indescribable rush of elation went through him. Glancing to the side, it seemed like the guys in white coats looked a wee bit disappointed.

Back at the base, guys gathered in front of their planes, all laughing like hell, shaking hands, clapping each other on the back and hugging. They were fighter pilots!

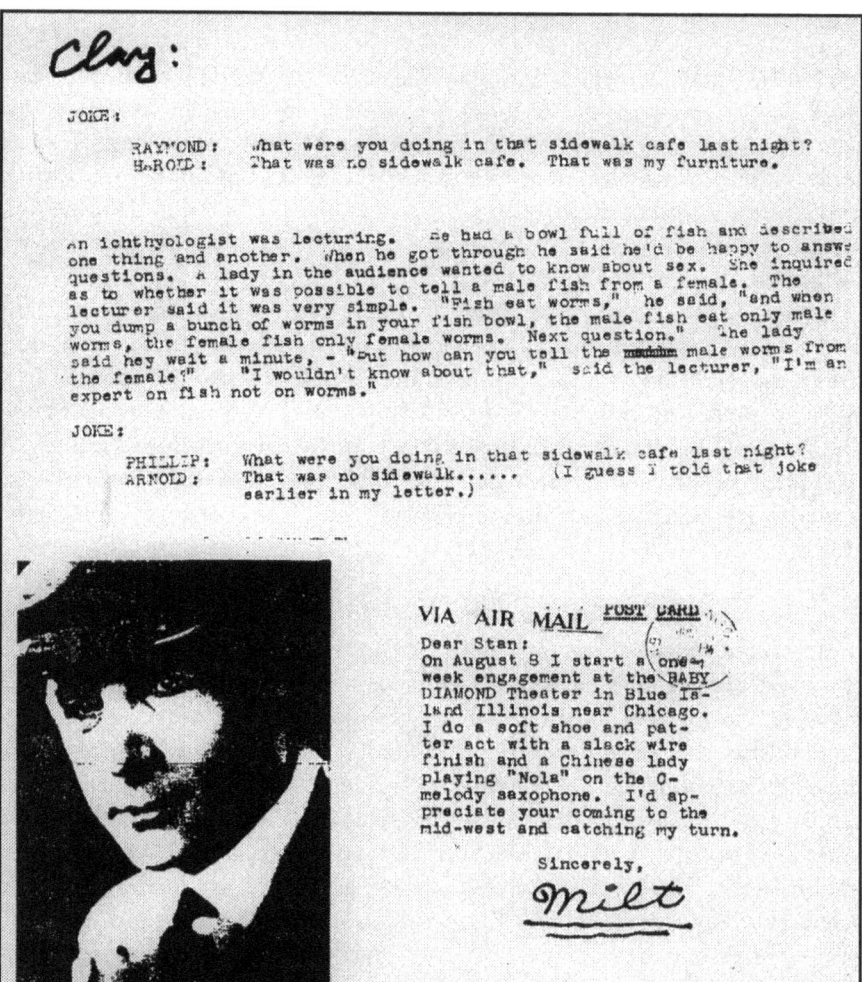

Clay:

JOKE:

RAYMOND: What were you doing in that sidewalk cafe last night?
HAROLD: That was no sidewalk cafe. That was my furniture.

An ichthyologist was lecturing. He had a bowl full of fish and described one thing and another. When he got through he said he'd be happy to answer questions. A lady in the audience wanted to know about sex. She inquired as to whether it was possible to tell a male fish from a female. The lecturer said it was very simple. "Fish eat worms," he said, "and when you dump a bunch of worms in your fish bowl, the male fish eat only male worms, the female fish only female worms. Next question." The lady said hey wait a minute, - "But how can you tell the male worms from the female?" "I wouldn't know about that," said the lecturer, "I'm an expert on fish not on worms."

JOKE:

PHILLIP: What were you doing in that sidewalk cafe last night?
ARNOLD: That was no sidewalk...... (I guess I told that joke earlier in my letter.)

VIA AIR MAIL POST CARD

Dear Stan:
On August 8 I start a one-week engagement at the BABY DIAMOND Theater in Blue Island Illinois near Chicago. I do a soft shoe and patter act with a slack wire finish and a Chinese lady playing "Nola" on the C-melody saxophone. I'd appreciate your coming to the mid-west and catching my turn.

Sincerely,

Milt

Chapter Eleven

Chapter Twelve

Gibby made another friend—"Wee Willie" Wilson. Mr. Five-by-Five—which meant he looked as wide as he was tall. In college he was a wrestler, and proved it soon after he and Gibby met. They wrestled and Willie pinned his new friend quickly. Then Gibby suggested boxing and there the results were reversed. So they had a firm foundation for a warm relationship. At the same time, he met Stavos, a close friend of Willie's.

Stavos suggested that the three of them go on a bike ride when they had a couple of free hours. It was a great idea. They rented bikes and rode along the main highway, stopping at the ubiquitous fruit stands to get a milk bottle full of orange juice for thirty-five cents, or some oranges after the owner of the stand cut several different oranges for them to sample.

They made this an almost daily custom because it was good exercise and also Stavos suffered from constipation, and found oranges a big help.

Gibby wanted to buy a car. He and Willie hitchhiked up to Tampa and scouted the used car lots. A 1933 Ford coupe caught their eye. One hundred dollars seemed like a fair price, even though the car had no lights, and gobbled as much oil as gas. When they drove it back to Melbourne, their buddies were all excited. That evening they took turns driving the coupe up and down the highway, shrieking like little kids. Apparently, most of them had never driven a car before, even though they were piloting 600-mile-an-hour fighter planes. The crewmen on the flight line heard about the car. One of them said, "Listen, whenever you need gas, come down to the flight line around midnight, and we'll fill you up with hundred octane." With gas available only with coupons, this was a real bonanza.

Training continued. They played follow-the-leader. Flying in a line, each pilot copied the maneuver of the plane ahead. They did loops, rolls, dives, spins and tight turns. They went into close formation, peeled out of it and then joined up again. There were gunnery and dive-bombing runs. Night flying. After a few weeks the Hellcat was as comfortable as an old shoe.

Willie suggested driving to Miami and Gibby liked the idea; they could go to Hialeah and play the horses. They had Sunday off, could leave Saturday night and return the next night. But they had no lights on the car. Gibby figured they could solve that. He parked by the side of the road until a truck came by, then swung in behind it and followed closely until he could no longer keep up. They also found a solution for the high rate of oil consumption. They pulled into gas stations that were closed for the night, found the sump of used oil that was always around, dipped into it with any vessel handy and poured it into the crankcase. Needless to say, their uniforms showed evidence of this tactic before long. At one gas station, they were conducting this activity when a window was raised in the house next door. A deep voice rang out: "I see ya there, and I got a shotgun! Get the hell out!" They departed promptly.

Willie had never been to a horse race, so Gibby undertook to educate him. "I don't like the big favorites or the big longshots. Stick with the medium odds. Four-to-one, to maybe eight-to-one. Any of those have a chance. It's all a matter of luck, so play the percentages."

"Got ya," said Willie.

The first race was won by a nag that went off at 60-1, and Willie started screaming and jumping up and down.

"What're you yelling for?" asked Gibby. "You didn't have that horse."

"Yeah, I did. How much did I win? How much did I win?" He turned to the crowd. "I had that horse! I knew he was gonna win! How much did I win?" he asked Gibby.

"How much did you bet?"

"Ten dollars."

"On his nose?"

"What does that mean?"

"Did you bet him to win?"

"Sure. I knew he was gonna win!"

"Then you've got about six hundred dollars." Gibby felt a little sick.

People began gathering around Willie. "What's good in the second?" they wanted to know.

"Let me look at the program," said Willie.

Chapter Twelve

"Jesus," said Gibby. "What're you doing now? Handicapping? You better be careful."

Willie ignored him, and gave the people a horse, which won at $22.40. They were all yelling like crazy and begging him to give them a horse in the third.

It was possibly the worst day of Gibby's life. Willie picked the winner of all eight races. And Gibby, whose pride prevented him from going with any of Willie's picks, got skunked.

"Where's a good restaurant around here?" Willie asked the crowd. "I want to take my buddy to dinner. Where can we get some steak and lobster?"

"I'm not hungry," said Gibby.

"Whatd'ya mean? We're gonna eat up a storm. I musta made five thousand dollars!"

Chapter Thirteen

They arrived back at the base the next morning to learn that they were going to be addressed by yet another envoy from Washington.

"Gentlemen," he said, "the big problem out there now is at night. The fleet is being attacked by night-flying bombers and torpedo planes, and we don't have a good way to stop them. Butch O'Hare put together a bunch of night-fighters, and they've had some fair results. The Navy department has decided to establish night-fighter training, and it's already in play. I'm here to ask for volunteers. The training lasts about six months, which means you'd have an extra six months before you'd be sent out to sea. Also, part of your training would be in New England, so you can take liberty in New York. It's a good deal."

The pilots looked at each other. If there was one common feeling among them it was that they all hated night flying! There were certainly enough dangers flying combat planes during the day. Why load the dice by flying in the dark? There was a sign-up sheet on the desk in the front of the room, but most of the traffic moved toward the rear, to the door.

Back in the hut, the guys were in paroxysms of laughter. "Night flying! Holy shit! Six more months in the States! Find me a good cemetery!"

Willie drifted in and put his arm around Gibby. "Hey, you and I are going to have fun in New York!"

Gibby turned, frowning. "Not me. I didn't sign up."

"That's O.K. I signed you up."

"What! You're joking!"

"No. I put you on the list. Honest."

Gibby ran as fast as he could, to the Ad building, and burst into the office of the flight officer. "There's been a mistake!" he yelled. "Somebody signed me up for night fighting, and I don't want it. Where's the Lieutenant that talked to us?"

The flight officer pointed out the window. "There he goes now." Gibby looked. A plane was just taking off. "I guess you're a night-fighter," said the flight officer.

Willie was not apologetic. "I did you a favor," he said. "You'll thank me. You know how most fighter pilots get killed? Anti-aircraft. They get shot down by anti-aircraft. Not enemy planes. Night-fighters don't have to worry about anti-aircraft."

"No. All they have to worry about is taking off and landing on a damn carrier at night."

"Piece of cake," said Willie.

Dear Gibby:

In the hospital I scribbled you off a quick post card. This trip I hope to give you a little more information. I am farting around with my typewriter for the first time in a month and am apt to be pretty much butter-fingers.

The enclosure shows my physician Doctor Rishigan Fishigan from Sishigan Michigan. He is an ambidextrous homosexual otorhinolaryngologist.

"ell, I had a pulmonary oedema. You'll recall from your expensive medical education at Marquette that the condition involves a flooding of the lungs with fluid and a poor halfwit dam near drowns. It hit me from clear out in left field. I was OK at 7:45 A.M. and in the hospital undergoing emergency treatment at 8:30. Electro-cardiagrams and other machinations showed that I'd had a slight infarction. This had to be treated as a bona fide heart attack so I was in the hospital a little over three weeks. I'm home now and must sit solemnly on my ass for another 21 days.

I've now had three coronary occlusions and this makes a guy somewhat thoughtful. Of course, on the cheery side I can't help reflecting that if I've survived three why can't I survive 127? It's Blue Cross's ass, not mine.

Wayne

When they left Melbourne, the night-fighters went to Vero Beach, which was just down the road a piece. And mostly they did night flying; taking off and landing, flying in formation, everything they did in day flying that was possible on a black night. It was especially daunting in central Florida because almost every night there was a thunderstorm, with lightning and lots of rain. Flying close formation was hairy since it was hard to see in heavy rain. Probably the Navy picked this spot because if you could fly at night under these conditions, you could do it anywhere.

And just to confuse things, Gibby's mother arrived to visit him. And it was apparent that it was not to be a short visit, since she announced that she had already rented a small house right next to the base. A couple of days later, she told Gibby that she had taken a job at a truck-stop near her new house. During these war years, employees were scarce and a strong woman who could cook was a welcome thing.

His mother made apple pie with a crust of pure butter. The family joke was that if you dropped one it would go right through the floor. But the truck drivers loved it. She bragged that business at the truck stop had picked up a lot because word of her apple pie had spread among the truck drivers.

Her house was located just across the fence from the end of the runway, and Gibby was concerned about it. "How do you get any sleep?" he asked her.

"No, it's wonderful," she said. "Every plane that goes over, I think it's you."

Almost every morning there were one or two empty chairs at the breakfast table in the mess hall. "Vertigo," was the usual answer. It was a mysterious and terrifying thing. Nobody really knew what it was, although there were constant warnings to avoid it. And everyone proclaimed they would never succumb to it. "It's disorientation," said the experts. "You don't know which is up and which is down, and finally you go into a spin, which is fatal." It happened generally on moonless nights; stars were no help, because they reflected in the water and it looked like sky.

In spite of the constant assertions that it would never happen to them, there continued to be the empty chairs at the breakfast table. And, eventually it happened to Gibby. He was flying in a tight formation. And suddenly he became alarmed. The whole formation had gone into a dive! He assumed it was a deliberate tactic to test their reactions. But they continued to dive! He was perfectly oriented—he could see the stars in the night sky! Finally he decided that the rest of the formation could dive into the ocean if they wanted to, but he would save himself, Goddamn it! He pulled back hard on the stick, and rose above the formation, bringing the nose up until he was flying straight and level. He had saved his life, and he took a deep breath of relief. But what had happened to the instruments? They had gone crazy! They indicated a situation that was directly contrary to what his senses were telling him. The senses he had lived by all his life! He knew absolutely and positively that he was flying on a level plane, but his airspeed was dropping off as if he were in a climb. As a matter of fact, it was getting dangerously close to stalling speed! Now he was in mortal conflict—what he knew absolutely, by the seat of his pants, was fighting the instruments he had learned to trust. Should he go against his basic instincts and dive into the ocean? It was a gut-wrenching struggle. But just as the plane began to shudder, a thought that had been fighting to come to the surface, emerged into his consciousness. Vertigo! He jammed forward on the stick and saw the airspeed needle stop and drop down to flying speed.

He was shaking like the proverbial leaf. My God, he had just faced vertigo! And beaten it. It was the first time in years he had considered the possibility of God.

```
                                    July 17
                                    1 0 5 8

Sweetest Bill:

I thought you might like the snapshot up above.  It is suitable

for placing in a medallion and wearing around the throat.

Your chatty letter was most enjoyable and informative and I

took the liberty of pinning it to the bulletin board in the

foyer of St. Chrysostom's Church.

A travelling salesman who had begged a bed from a farmer was unable
to get to sleep.  (There's a lot of opening build-up to this
but I'm starting with these two guys in the same bed.)  The farmer
couldn't sleep either.   He said, "When my wife and I are wakeful we
play a variation of football that generally works."    Salesman: "How
does it go?".  Farmer: "Well, whoever lets a fart calls it a touch-
down and gives himself 12 points. Shall we start?"    The salesman
achieved a fart and was          awarded a touchdown.  The farmer re-
taliated in a moment.   The game went on.  Pretty quick the score was
24 to 24.  Then the farmer - after a tremendous effort -          screamed
like a tiger.  "I shit!" he howled.  "I shit all over!"   The salesman
said, "Well, in that case I guess you forfeit the game."    "The hell
I do," shouted the farmer, "That's  the end of the first quarter.
Now we change sides!"
                                                    Wayne
```

The next afternoon, he drove over to see his mother. She was back from work and he still had an hour or so before he had to fly.

"You want fruit?" she said. "I got a lot of fruit." She showed him two large bags of grapefruit and oranges. They were so heavy Gibby could hardly lift them. "Where did you get all these?" he asked.

"In the big place down there, where they got all the fruit."

"You mean the warehouse down the road?"

"Yeah."

"What'd it cost you?"

She laughed, mischievously. "A quarter."

"What? For all this?"

"Yeah. I went in and there was a man on a ladder. And I told him I wanted a few oranges. So he says leave a quarter and take as many as I could carry. So I put down a quarter and filled up two bags. He wasn't watching."

"Jesus. How did you get them here?"

"A truck driver stopped, and took me home. And he took the bags for me inside. He says he loves my apple pie."

"Well, you got a few oranges."

"Yeah. I did good, no?"

They both laughed until they cried.

Chapter Fourteen

He was transferred to Westerly, Rhode Island, the first time he had ever seen New England. The trees were painted in startling colors. The winter beaches were blustery and deserted. He was in love with the place! They flew, of course, day and night, but it was less regimented, somehow. They were encouraged to take solo flights, anywhere they liked. They investigated Block Island, which was just off the base, Long Island, even New York. At night they intercepted commercial planes and flew close beside them, giving the passengers inside something to talk about. There was an army field nearby and during the day they played and had mock dogfights with the P-47s.

His mother, ever resourceful, found her own way. She had a little money, augmented by what she'd earned at the truck stop, and she came by bus to Westerly and put up at a hotel. A few days later, she had a job at a shop on Long Island.

Willie was right: They had fun on liberty in New York. Gibby's routine was to take the train into the city, get a nice hotel room and cruise the bars for girls. They were pretty easy to get. His wings shone enticingly on his uniform and most girls' boyfriends were away in the service. And it eased the sense of betrayal to go to bed with an aviator who might never make it through the war. It was a time of abandon. All you needed was a lively place and enough booze.

He was in the lounge, listening to the radio. American soldiers had just stormed the beaches of Normandy. A workman in overalls came in and sort of sneered. "Listening about the invasion, huh? You'll never go over."

"You probably won't either," said Gibby.

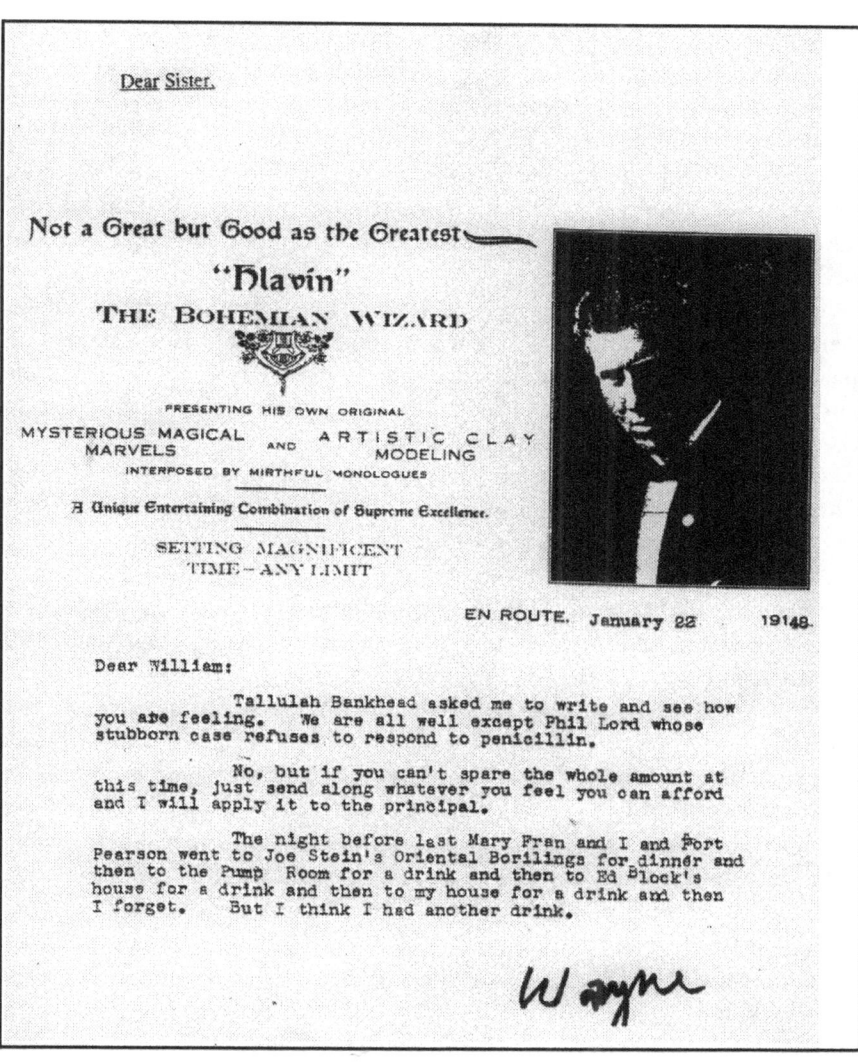

They were sent to Charlestown, which was about ten miles up the coast toward Providence, and everything changed a lot. The Hellcats now had radar. It was in a nacelle, looking like a big blue teardrop in the right wing. And now it was all about interceptions; the meat and potatoes of their future job at sea. It went like this: A twin-engine plane was dispatched out to sea. It represented a "bogey" (an enemy plane). Then the fighters were sent out. The ship's radar saw the "bogey," and directed one of the fighter planes to intercept it. The radar supplied information regarding the target's heading and altitude, and the fighter tracked it.

When the fighter was within about twenty miles of the target, his own radar took over, and the fighter closed the distance. When it was really close, a gun-sight framed the target and the pilot pulled the trigger, and announced, "Splash, one bogey!"

Actually, when the fighter plane was close behind the target, the pilot of the target plane turned on his lights to avoid getting his tail cut off. The goal was to have each fighter pilot complete 300 interceptions before he was sent out.

Porter Hartman was one of the new ensigns. He was a quiet fellow, slender and aristocratic, from a good Eastern family. He didn't stand out, particularly. Until one day, when playing volleyball, he took a tumble and bruised his knee rather badly. The other guys advised him to go to the sickbay so they could stop the bleeding.

Gibby saw him later, in the shower, and asked how he was doing. Porter smiled strangely. "I don't know. They examined me and said that my reflexes weren't good. I'm grounded."

"For how long?"

Porter shook his head. "Maybe permanently."

Gibby stared at him as if he'd announced he had leprosy. The word spread around the base like wildfire, and the reaction was peculiar. Everyone felt sorry for him, of course, but they avoided him too. It was like he was contagious. The tragedy that had befallen him was too nightmarish to contemplate, and it was like if people got too close, it might rub off on them. Getting washed out was bad enough, but somehow getting your wings and then losing them seemed worse. Porter came into the bar like everyone else, but people would pat him on the back and then sit several stools away from him. When he entered a room, the conversation dropped a notch.

It was confirmed: Porter was permanently grounded. He could still wear his wings, but he couldn't fly. The Navy Department had been contacted and had been asked to issue new orders for him, but so far, nothing had come through.

The casualty rate in night-fighter training was twenty-five-percent. One in four. Lots of bodies were sent home. And each body, by regulations, had to be accompanied by an officer of like rank. After a time, one of the brass came up with the bright idea of having Porter accompany the bodies instead of taking a flyer out of training. He fulfilled the regulations—he was an officer of the same rank as the ensign who'd died. The fact that he couldn't fly was merely a technicality that no one needed to know.

And pretty soon there was an accident, a fatal one. And Porter went in to the officer in charge to get his instructions for taking the body home.

"Be serious. Don't smile a lot when the family is around. Don't tell jokes. Answer when you're spoken to but maintain your dignity. They don't want a comedian. And the most important thing—stay close to the body at all times. Very important not to lose the body!"

When Porter got back from his trip, people were curious. They wanted to know how it went. And he was not particularly anxious to discuss it. But they probed and little by little, it came out. The body was put in the baggage car, and the train made its way to Texas where the family lived. On the way, he ran into a rich guy from Texas who was impressed with the young fighter pilot, and they became close. They had drinks in the dining car, and the rich guy proposed introducing Porter to Miss Texas, whom the rich guy knew. Anyway, Porter met her after the funeral, and slept with her before boarding the train for home.

The guys were awed, and happy for Porter, in a way. After all, when a guy experiences a misfortune like his, he deserves all the breaks he can get.

They were placed into flight groups, which were to subsist even after they went into combat. The head guy of Gibby's group was Macintosh, a burly guy who had played center for the Giants. Then there was Burton, a laconic, funny guy from New Mexico, Ellison, a tall Swede, "Wee Willie," "Stub," and Gibby.

When the night's flying was over, the four men joined up and flew for an hour or so in the breaking daylight, for what reason no one knew. But it was routine. And this flight was possibly the most dangerous of them all. They didn't know why, but flying at this time of day made them all extremely sleepy. Gibby would nod off any number of times and awaken terrified to find himself in formation, his left wing an inch or two from the wing beside him.

On this particular morning, the fog had dropped down and was hugging the water. Macintosh led them on a sort of aimless cruise in the heavy haze, apparently trying to find a break where he could see the water or ground, and find his way back to the base.

Then Gibby saw tree tops! Mac and Burton, who was flying stepped-down on Mac's left, and Gibby, stepped-down on Mac's right, pulled up over them, missing them by inches. Ellison, who was stepped-down on Gibby's right, disappeared. He'd hit the trees, they found out when they returned to base, and was gone. He was now in Porter's hands.

Chapter Fourteen

Saturday the 3rd

Old Pal,

I am propped up in bed and can scribble. The doctor says I am making satisfactory progress. However, all heart cases have to be treated as critical cases and I may have to be on my back for some weeks to come. For a solid week I wore an oxygen contraption and felt high like I was full of martinis. I am in a double room and this morning at four they brought in a guy who promptly died before my eyes. He had a heart attack but good. There was considerable traffic in and out of the room and everybody who left, tiptoed out solemnly and respectfully, leaving me in the room with my quiet companion.

Wayne

Chapter Fifteen

Mac took the loss of Ellison hard, apparently feeling that it was his fault. He should have made sure he was over the water instead of the trees when he led the descent. Anyway, his disposition seemed to change, and he appeared to lose his appetite for flying after that, keeping himself and Burton, his closest friend, off the flight roster whenever possible.

Porter did accompany Ellison home to Chicago, and the rest of the guys could hardly wait to hear what experiences he might have had on the trip. He didn't disappoint them, although again he was diffident about recounting them. He was on the train with the body, and again he met a well-to-do businessman who was anxious to show his patriotic appreciation to this brave fighter pilot. The man's destination was the west coast, but he said he knew of the world's finest brothel, and it was in Chicago. They arrived in Chicago the night before the funeral, and the businessman insisted that they go to the whorehouse that night. Porter refused politely, saying that it was his duty to remain with the body. No problem, said the businessman.

He hired a hearse and they drove to the bawdy house with the corpse in the rear. The rich guy knew the madam and arranged for a room to stash the body while he and Porter enjoyed the offerings of the establishment.

The army airbase next door made a request to the night-fighters. The army was training anti-aircraft teams, and wanted the night-fighters to play the enemy. They wanted them to stage a mock night attack on the army airfield and give the men who manned the searchlights some practice at defending the base.

Gibby was sent over, together with "Wee Willie" and several others. Gibby and Willie were to attack the first group of searchlights at the edge of the base. They kept in radio contact so they could alternate their dives and not both attack at the same time. Gibby dove and was enveloped in blinding light. He called Willie and told him to be very careful; it was impossible to see when the lights hit you and to watch his altimeter so that he could pull up in time. "Gotcha," said Willie.

When he returned to the base, he got the news he most feared. Willie had gone in. The next morning he stared at Willie's empty chair at the breakfast table.

They did some day flying so that they could maintain their skills, like gunnery. Gibby, in an opposite end run, ducked under the target plane and angled upward to shoot at the sleeve. Somehow he hit the connection between the rope and the sleeve and the rope, suddenly free, whipped down and wrapped around his right wing, several times. It happened in a millisecond. His aileron was wrapped completely, so he couldn't bank the plane. He went into a dive and shook the wings as well as he could, with the stick. He climbed and did the same. No soap. He called the instructor and explained the dilemma. In a couple of minutes Lt. Gruder was flying at his side. The instructor talked to him.

"Hey, you got a problem, don't you? I might be able to slide my wing . . . No, I better not . . . Christ, I don't know . . . But don't go into any dives, you might spin and then you'd be up shit creek."

They flew along together. Gibby saw the Lieutenant peering at his wing, then shaking his head. "Listen, I'm going to try it. Can you fly straight and level and steady for a couple of minutes?" Gibby nodded. "Okay now, steady . . . Here I come . . ."

Gibby watched the instructor's wing inch toward his and then turned his attention to keeping the plane absolutely steady. The wing was nearing the rope . . . Gibby looked ahead. Thoughts streamed through his mind. What a stupid thing to happen. It wasn't going to work. What a ridiculous way to go. One in four, one in four. Porter would take him home. Where was his home, anyway? When he looked back, he saw the instructor's wing poking at the rope, like an inquisitive snake. It pulled away and then came back. Poke, poke . . . the pitot tube on the tip of the wing got under a loop of rope. Then Gruder pulled up abruptly as his plane shot ahead.

The loop pulled loose. The end of the rope went over the front of the wing. The wind caught it, and blew it toward the rear. The rope unwound and disappeared. When Gruder slowed and came back to him, Gibby waved and blew the instructor a kiss.

Porter didn't come around much at this time, except to pick up a body or report after a delivery. The scuttlebutt was that he had a girlfriend and they spent a lot of time at the beach.

Gibby's mother was doing fine. She took a bus out to Long Island every day and dusted the antiques in the shop where she worked.

The time was getting short before they would be sent out to sea. They talked about it a lot when they were together. "I wonder how hard it is to get to be an ace?" said "Stub." "What is an ace, anyway? Five planes?"

"Yeah."

Mac spoke. "I'll bet anybody a hundred bucks they don't get five planes." He looked around the room. Nobody took the bet.

The last hurdle was carrier landings. A strip had been spread out on the runway, roughly the dimensions of a carrier. At the landing area were restraining cables that would stop their momentum when they hooked onto them.

"Listen," said the instructor, "this will actually be harder than landing on a real carrier, because at sea the ship heads into the wind and there's twenty knots of wind coming over the deck against you. This makes the landing and the takeoff shorter. There's hardly any wind at all out here."

The instructor hadn't lied. The constrained space of the landing area made it tough and the jerk of the cables was violent because of the lack of a headwind. But finally they each completed six landings and then hoped to hell it was easier on a real carrier.

They received two replacements for Wee Willie and Ellison: Thompson, another funny guy who was something of a cartoonist, and Bruno, who smoked cigars when he was flying and was altogether cool. They had been trained at another base and were at the same stage as Mac's group.

This was it! Time to ship out! No more training, no more liberties in New York, the Navy was calling their marker! They piled into the back of a pick-up, with their bags and possessions and rode out of the base. Bouncing along a dirt road, they looked up to the left. On a hill above them there was a little white house. On the front porch, in deck chairs, sat Porter and a gorgeous blonde. Porter held a tall glass and was smoking a cigar. When he saw the pick-up, he stood and waved. Gibby and his friends waved back. As they bounded away, somebody said: "God! That poor son-of-a-bitch!"

The itinerary was simple: A train to Los Angeles, where they joined other groups, some from Charlestown, and some from other bases; from

> Saturday
>
> Dear old Gibby,
>
> Mary Fran overheard a group of my doctors discussing my case out in the hall. One was saying gravely, "It's between Wayne and his maker now."
>
> I believe the opinion in the hospital is that this last attack damaged my wits. Guys in white jackets hold up a forefinger and say "What is this?"
>
> "Eleanor Roosevelt". "Two!" I shout.
>
> "Right," they say.
>
> But I am reassured that if I have weathered two heart attacks why can't I weather a dozen? It's Blue Cross's ass, not mine.
>
> Best wishes,
> Wayne

there they flew to Hawaii. Before the plane left they had a couple of hours for sociability, which, of course, they spent in the bar. The plane took off, but soon returned to L.A. because of engine trouble. Most of the pilots thought they were already in Hawaii.

Hawaii! It was a revelation to most of them, being much more familiar with cornfields than pineapple groves. On the bus they passed Pearl Harbor, which still showed vestiges of the Japanese attack. Their destination was Barber's Point in the northernmost part of the big island.

If they thought Melbourne was a vacation spot, Barber's Point was a resort. The people stationed there had it whipped, and knew it. Every Saturday night there was a dance, and the most beautiful girls on the island, Caucasian and Hawaiian, attended. There were food and drinks, and everybody got smashed. There was also a fabulous beach that was reached by descending a trail lined with flowers and a workshop where people did projects and crafts. Incidentally, it was also an airbase. There were fighter planes and the night-fighters were expected to fly solo at least three nights a week to keep their hand in.

By coincidence, Della was now in the USO and stationed at an army base not far from Barber's Point. Gibby called her and they agreed to meet the next afternoon in Honolulu. When they got together, they decided to have a drink, but that was not as easy as it sounds. Every respectable bar had lines of servicemen waiting to get in. When they did finally wait it out and get inside, their drinks tasted like shoe polish.

"This is almost as bad as the chicken-fried steak in Corpus, isn't it?" said Gibby.

"I guess wartime is not the time for gourmet dining."

But Gibby had a job for Della. He dug a bunch of letters from his pocket. "There's twenty of them, all addressed. Put stamps on 'em and send one a week to Ma. It'll look like I'm in Hawaii the whole time. I don't know when we're going out, but it should be soon."

"O.K., but don't worry. She's out of red medicine."

It was great seeing Della, and when he flew at night he always buzzed her base as a greeting.

They were in Hawaii about three weeks and built a beautiful tan, then boarded a ship for Guam. On the way they crossed the equator and all agreed it was not nearly as hot as Corpus.

Chapter Fifteen 65

Chapter Sixteen

The thing they first noticed about Guam was that all the trees were cut off about five feet above the ground, as if with a giant cleaver. "The Navy's big guns did that," they were told.

If Hawaii was a sophisticated resort, Guam was back to the primitive. The main activities for the ensigns were swimming in the turquoise water and eating coconuts. One of the most satisfying things Gibby ever learned was how to open a coconut. A knife was no good, a machete or even a hatchet was useless. A man needed a piece of hardwood about half the length of a baseball bat, sharpened at each end. One end was driven into the ground; the iron-shelled coconut was held in both hands and the side of it was banged on the sharp end of the stick that pointed upward until a split occurred in the shell. Then the point of the stick was inserted in the split and the coconut was rotated and banged until the shell came off. Now you had the inner part of the coconut one sees in the supermarket.

People were scoring 100-proof alcohol, where, no one knew. But it appeared frequently and some were getting very high. Burton was sitting on the floor, a clay pot between his legs. In the pot were lime juice, orange juice, ice and coconut milk. He picked up a bottle of alcohol from the floor beside him. "Now," he said, "this is the most important part. One drop too much and the whole thing is ruined." He put his other hand over his eyes and poured the whole bottle into the pot. "Perfect," he yelled. "Absolutely perfect!" Guys, laughing, advanced with their cups and filled up. And so it went. One night, the guys, already loaded, hitched a ride on a dynamite truck, and shouted with glee as they tossed case after case of dynamite off the speeding pick-up.

The word was that they were on the island to wait for a ship to take them aboard. And they were ready. They'd had all the training they could stand and they felt perfectly confident to meet the challenges ahead. They talked about it every spare moment. They speculated on what it would be like to be in a dogfight with a Zero, or strafe a ship, or bomb an airport

After three weeks on Guam they were taken aboard a boat that would take them to their ship—the *Hornet*. They were excited as hell as they approached the ladder that led up to the main deck of that majestic ship, and they didn't forget to salute the ship's officer and the flag as they climbed aboard.

The *Hornet* was more than five hundred feet long, the flagship of Admiral Halsey, and carried over three thousand seamen. It was like a floating, fighting hotel! After they were shown to their bunks (the ensigns were in a sort of dormitory that held twelve), they wandered around the ship. Coming up on the flight deck, they became aware that the *Hornet* was anchored amidst a flotilla of ships that seemed to spread to the horizon: carriers, battleships, cruisers, destroyers and a myriad of service vessels. If they'd had more experience in the Navy, they might have suspected that something special, something big was in the works. That night, after dinner, when they returned to the flight deck, the ships had turned on their lights and it looked like they were in the middle of a great city.

The next few days there was not much to do except to familiarize themselves with their new home: The hangar deck, where the planes were stored and repaired; the wardroom, where they would eat their meals and play cards; the ready room, where they would suit up for flights and hang out; the flight deck, where the planes came up on elevators to take off, and taken down after landing. And for Gibby and all the guys like him, who were never quite sure of where they were at any given moment, they learned of the miracle of the radio navigation system. There was a transmitter at the highest point of the ship that rotated constantly, sending out a different letter in Morse code every fifteen degrees. The plan of this rotation was changed every few days so that it was difficult for the enemy to steal, but all the pilots had the latest edition clipped to their navigation board. In operation it was simple. The pilots tuned in, heard a letter and knew immediately where they were in relation to the ship.

At daybreak, February 13, 1945, the pilots awoke to the sound of anchor chains being raised. They hurried into their clothes and went up on deck. The sight was mind-blowing. Every ship in the harbor was on the move! The city was going out to sea! All the ships were going in the same direction but they were gradually spreading apart to give each other room to maneuver.

There was a voice on the loudspeaker, ordering all flying officers to go to the wardroom immediately.

The wardroom was full of chairs, and filling up quickly. There were at least two hundred airmen assembled when an officer took his place at the front of the room. He looked over his audience for a few seconds, then spoke. "Gentlemen," he said, "I am Lieutenant Weider. Now that we are underway, I can tell you about our mission." He paused for a moment or two. "About three years ago, Jimmy Doolittle took off with his B-25s from this very same ship and attacked Tokyo. That's where we're going. Three days from now we will be part of the first carrier plane raid on Tokyo." Officers turned and looked at one another. Some seemed delighted, some worried, some shocked. "I'm sure you are aware of the enormous number of vessels in this harbor. We have eight major carriers, sixteen battleships and twelve hundred planes. The greatest armada in history.

"According to our intelligence, the Japanese have stationed the bulk of their airforce around the city of Tokyo. When we begin the attack, they will undoubtedly send all their fighters up to meet us, and we should have very good hunting.

"Now, a little advice: If you've got a cold, don't fly. If you're constipated, don't fly. If you've changed your mind about shedding blood, come see me. Finally, I suggest that you inspect your airplanes and make sure they are ready for combat. Dismissed."

Down on the hangar deck, the night-fighters stood in a group around one of their planes. Burton said, "I got a cold, I'm constipated and a little bit yella." Then he went closer to the plane. "Y'know, I can tell if a plane is any good the same way you pick a watermelon." He knocked on the side of the plane and it made a hollow sound. "This one is O.K." But the excitement and sense of anticipation permeated the ship. Even the sailors took it on. Everyone seemed infused with a certain heightened awareness. Whatever one did, he did with extra vigor. We were going to engage the enemy in his lair. Tokyo! Who'd expected that we would even see it?

And, as it turned out, the night-fighters were not going to see it. They were slated for patrol duty around the ships. While the other planes were carrying the ball against Tokyo, they would be playing defense, guarding the fleet against a counterattack. They were disappointed, but were told they had a duty as important as the others.

Mac gave them some news. "Listen," he said, "I've been talking to some of the regular Navy guys. They say we shouldn't count on being used very much while we're out here. They say that the brass is leery of night-fighters. They got no confidence in 'em. And another thing—the one thing they're scared of more than anything else in the world, is showing a light on board at night. They figure the night-fighters might require a light of some kind. And that's strictly taboo. Even lighting a cigarette on deck at night will get you court-martialed."

Great! They were relegated to sitting on their asses for the next six months while the other pilots fought the war. Morale was low among the night-fighters.

Patrol duty was to be shared among the night-fighters of four carriers, Mac's group being the first. They took off at six-thirty, a half-hour after the Tokyo-bound planes took off. They spaced themselves and patrolled the fleet, maintaining contact with the radar room, waiting for the word that an enemy plane might be coming out to attack, whereupon they would go into their well-rehearsed interception mode. But the hours passed, and their radios were silent. Though they scoured the heavens for any speck that might be an enemy plane, the skies held nothing but clouds. After three hours they were told to come back to the ship. The fleet turned into the wind preparatory to taking them aboard, and allowing the next group of patrollers to take off.

Gibby and the rest of the group were frustrated. They had expected all hell to break loose, and nothing had happened. They repaired to the wardroom for coffee and something to eat. "What the hell happened?" said "Stub."

"Nothing."

"Where were all the Jap planes?"

"Probably the other guys shot 'em all down."

"Yeah, there's probably fifty aces out there."

"Son-of-a-bitch."

But when the first group of day-fighters came in, they had very little to report. "We strafed buildings and a train. Some guys dropped a few bombs . . ."

"But no planes?"

"Not a one. We were expecting a million of 'em, but there weren't any. Anywhere."

"Christ, where were they?"

Chapter Sixteen

"God knows. Maybe they got smart and kept 'em on the ground."

"Sneaky bastards."

That evening a bunch of the pilots gathered in the ready room, giddy with the release of tension after a nerve-wracking day. "Hey, y'know what the movie is tonight? *Thirty Seconds over Tokyo*".

"Shit, I just spent two and a half hours over it!"

Another guy had a letter. "It's a bill. He says If I don't pay it, I'm in a lot of trouble. Jesus, I'm scared."

Chapter Seventeen

The *Hornet* with its cargo of frustrated pilots turned south and sailed away from Japan. The whereabouts of the Japanese air force was still a mystery. The night-fighters had a meeting on the flight deck with a Landing Signal officer. "Listen, if you guys ever fly at night—which I doubt . . ."

"Yeah, we heard," said Mac.

"Right. These guys are as jittery as a virgin in a whorehouse about showing a light at night. But, in case you do fly, I want to brief you on how to make a landing on this ship. Now, listen up . . .

"There's a big red light recessed in the center of the flight deck. The only place you can see it is if you're directly over it. It can't be seen from the water, get it?" They all nodded. "O.K., when you return to the ship, you fly over it and see the light. Then, check the wake so you see how the ship is headed. Got it? You fly in that direction for three minutes. Then you turn left ninety degrees and fly for one minute. Then you turn left again ninety degrees and you're flying parallel to the ship, but in the opposite direction ... everybody understand? You fly until you see a flash of light from the ship. There's a guy on the flight deck with a gun-light, and he aims it right at you and gives you one flash. That's your signal to turn toward the ship. You should be in perfect position to make your final turn for your landing. At that point, you'll see me. I'll be in a two-sided tent, wearing a fluorescent suit and lit by a light at my feet. I'll have two paddles, also fluorescent. Pay very close attention now. If I hold them at a forty-five-degree angle toward the deck, you're too low. If I point them up over my head, you're too high. If I do the breast stroke, you're too slow. When I bang my right leg, you're too fast. When I slash the right one across my neck, you cut the gun. At that point you'll see lights along the sides of the landing area. They come out of slits pointed seventeen degrees upward. They can be seen at that one spot and no other. If I wave the paddles back and forth over my head, that's a wave-off and you gotta go around again. Go it? If you ignore a wave-off and land, it's a court-martial. Want me to go over it again?" They all shook their heads. They got it.

Gibby was awakened by somebody shaking his shoulder. "Get up to the ready room right now," said the unknown person. Gibby looked at his watch. Almost two a.m. He got into his clothes and made his way to the ready room, which was right next to the flight deck. Mac and Burton were already there, sitting in the padded seats. In a moment, Thompson came in and sat down. Lt. Weathers, a radar officer, was standing at the front, beside a blackboard.

"Look," he said. "An hour ago, we intercepted a message from the Japanese and decoded it. It looks like the entire Jap airforce is in Kyushu. That's one of three tiny islands off the Eastern tip of Japan. The Admiral wants you night-fighters to go and confirm this information." He turned to the blackboard and made a quick, rough outline of Japan, and circled the left tip. "That's Kyushu. Now, the weather is bad. There's a heavy storm out there, and we also got word from radar that enemy planes are coming toward us. There will probably be anti-aircraft from some of our other ships.

"When you take off don't try to join up. Proceed on your own to Kyushu. You will show no lights. And at the crack of dawn, get the hell out of there. There's a thousand planes on that field. Good luck, and may God have mercy on your souls."

They got into their flight gear and went out on deck. There sure as hell was a big storm out there, with thunder and lightning. And there was also anti-aircraft fire coming from some of the surrounding ships.

They were catapulted from the ship, one at a time. Gibby was third to go, with Thompson behind him. He was scared. Navigation was not his strong suit. As a matter of fact he was known to get lost at times. Now he was flying to a dot three hundred miles away, all alone, at night, in bad weather, to find a thousand planes, all of whom would love to shoot him to pieces. And they had been warned against using the radio.

He flew in silence, except for the drone of the engine, for almost an hour, then decided to turn on his radar. Holy shit! On the screen was the outline of a land mass looking remarkably like the left side of the map the radar officer had drawn on the blackboard. He flew toward it. In a few minutes he was passing over a line of mountains, and down in the valley before him was . . . Broadway!

An airfield, lit up like a Christmas tree, with planes flying around it with their light on too. Just ahead were the lights of an enemy plane. He pressed forward on the throttle and got behind it. From the rear of the plane came a blinker, flashing at him. Probably the rear gunner saying, "Turn on your Goddamn lights, stupid!"

Gibby charged his guns with his right foot, got the plane in his sights and pulled the trigger. The enemy plane pulled straight up, did a wing-over and then dove, straight down. Gibby's plane rocked violently. He assumed it was the turbulence of the other plane coming so close. He sat there with his legs shaking.

Another plane, a large bomber, went by, and Gibby got on him and pulled the trigger. A blast of blinding ferocity lit the sky. It was a sight like nothing he had ever seen! Five hundred gallons of gasoline, exploding in a black night!

His radio came on, with Mac's voice: "Who did that?"

Gibby answered, "It was me, Winkler."

Gibby's feet were bouncing on the pedals, and his knees were wobbling like crazy. A ball of fire exploded on the other side of the field. Probably Mac, thought Gibby.

Another bomber flew over him, from the opposite direction. Gibby made a U-turn, and went after him, but wondered if he could shoot, shaking as badly as he was. He got behind the bomber but was going too fast, and slid under him. He slowed down and made another approach, still too fast, and slid under the enemy plane again. He came back and this time was in good position. His finger was on the trigger, about to shoot, when the plane in front of him blew up!

Mac's voice was on the radio. "Was that you, again, Winkler?"

"No," said Gibby. "I was just about to shoot. But it blew up."

"That was me," said Thompson.

Gibby sat there and shook. The two of them had been maneuvering under that plane in the blackness, probably inches from each other. Christ!

Thompson got another plane and then there was another ball of fire on the other side of the field, and abruptly the whole airfield shut down. All the lights went off. No more planes could be seen.

Mac was on the radio. "Strafe the field," he said. They began to dive, spraying the planes parked below with their fifty calibers, and continued until light began to show in the East. "Join up," said Mac. "We're done here."

Gibby realized, with a start, that he didn't know where the rendezvous was supposed to take place. He began wandering around the sky, disregarding the thousand enemy planes below. Finally, he used the radio. "Fellas, where we supposed to join up?" But the next moment he saw that his three mates had come to find him. They went by him with their lights on, and he happily swung into his proper place.

Daylight was well established when they got back to the carrier. One by one they landed. Gibby taxied up to his mechanic and rolled back his canopy. The guy was looking at his right wing and yelling: "Hey, what happened to your fuckin' wing?"

"Why? What's wrong?"

"Look at it, for Christ sakes!"

Gibby got out and stood on the wing. There was a depression in the middle of it as big as a bathtub! "God," he said, "the guy hit me!"

The night-fighters got together, and were told to go up to the radar room to get debriefed. They were as high as kites. They laughed at anything said. Lt. Weathers, the officer who briefed them in the ready room before the flight was now doing the debriefing. He asked them about the mission, and they all began yelling at once, laughing and gesturing as if they were on grass. "Whoa! Whoa!" said the Lt. "Calm down." One by one they told their stories, laughing like fools, as Weathers took notes. When it was Gibby's turn, he told about the first enemy plane he attacked, and the collision. "I thought it was his slipstream, but he actually hit me!"

"I saw him crash," said Thompson.

"Really?" said Gibby. "He crashed?"

"Yeah, I was just coming up on the field, and I saw tracers—I didn't know they were yours. But I saw the other plane dive, and then he crashed."

"Then you got two," said Mac.

"I guess so."

"You strafed the field," said Weathers. "How high were you when you started?"

"At the top," said Burton.

"And where did you finish?"

"At the bottom!" They all yelled, and broke up.

The location of the enemy confirmed, fighters from all the carriers were on their way. They caught the Japanese planes taking off and destroyed a great number of them.

> Dear Patient Tyler,
>
> We are asking you to discontinue your habit of using the hot buttered pocketbook rolls as a device for self-abuse.
>
> The Hospital Management

Chapter Eighteen

The Admiral was now in love with the "Black Chickens" (code for night-fighters) and vowed he would use them whenever possible. They flew almost every other night, on patrol, alternating with those of the *Bennington*, which sailed next to them.

Every seven or eight days the *Hornet* turned south and sailed away from the combat zone to refuel and take on supplies and mail. It took about twelve hours en route and twelve hours to refuel. This was essentially a day off for the pilots. The evening before the refueling there was a traditional ceremony. A gunnysack was brought out into the dormitory room where all the fighter pilots were assembled. Two men held the sack at the neck to make an aperture of four to five inches. Then each pilot plunged a hand through the hole to the bunch of whiskey bottles at the bottom. You pulled out a bottle, sight unseen. Whatever you pulled out was yours, to do with at your pleasure. Gibby always got Three Feathers or Four Roses, cheap booze, while others retrieved Jack Daniels or Wild Turkey. But what the hell, it all tasted like whiskey and it all got you drunk. People drank, and opened their mail and presents, and laughed a lot and then went to bed to sleep it off. We understood that this event was sanctioned by the Captain, but not by the Admiral.

One day during refueling, General Quarters sounded. Somehow, enemy planes were in the vicinity. The loudspeakers announced that a "Scramble" was ordered. A scramble meant that planes were on the flight deck and pilots were to get into their gear, grab the first empty plane available, and take off. Then they would be directed by the radar officers. Pilots, most of them hung over from the evening before, rushed and stumbled to the planes. "Stub," always an enthusiastic drinker, apparently stumbled more than most, and was noticed by the Admiral who ordered him removed from his plane and thrown into the brig. There was also a rumor of court-martial, but it wasn't carried out, mostly because of the intercession of the Captain.

Speaking of "Stub," he carried a deep, dark secret all through training and into combat; he got sick every time he flew. This was a washout sin in training and probably dischargeable after. But he always got the sympathy of the mechanics and they would help him clean out the cockpit after he threw up, and they kept their mouth shut.

The brass had another job for the night-fighters. The beaches of Japan were going to be photographed in detail, in preparation for a possible invasion. The photo planes were going to fly low over the coast, shooting film, while the night-fighters dove on the anti-aircraft installations to divert attention from the low-flying photographers. It had to be completely co-coordinated. The pilot from the lead photo plane called Mac when they were ready to begin their run and Mac signaled his boys to begin their dives.

It was hairy. The anti-aircraft fire came up in little balls of flame, getting bigger as they got closer and then went by with a whoosh. They continued their dives for a couple of hours, miraculously without being hit, and then went back to the ship.

April 1, 1945—The invasion of Okinawa. Gibby and Thompson were sent to Buckner Bay to patrol the ships that had delivered the invasion force, against the possibility of Kamikazes. At dusk the two pilots flew over Buckner Bay and every one of the 1,500 ships anchored there opened fire on them. They got out of there in a hurry and Gibby got on the radio to the *Hornet*: "These guys are shooting at us! Can you call the command out here, and get 'em to stop? Tell 'em we're here to protect them, for Christ sake!"

"Will do. Roger and out."

The two pilots orbited for a few minutes, then returned to the Bay. Again, they met a barrage of friendly fire. Gibby was beside himself. "They're still trying to kill us, for God's sake!" he radioed. "If they don't quit, we're leaving and going back to the ship! Tell 'em that."

After a few minutes, the firing stopped, and then two Japanese planes came over the Bay. Thompson saw them first and peeled off after them. He shot the first one down and then pulled up, to give Gibby a chance. Gibby took it and downed the second one.

But he was in trouble. His engine was missing. He and Thompson somehow got separated heading back to the ship. His engine began missing so badly he slid his canopy back in preparation to ditch the plane in the sea. He radioed Thompson and told him the situation. Thompson called the radar room and asked if they could vector him onto Gibby's plane so he could keep track of him. They said they would try. Another problem—his radio navigation system quit! He could no longer get his heading to the ship. He called the ship and they said they would give him a constant vector. Gibby said O.K., but that if he made it back, he couldn't take a wave-off, that he was afraid if he gunned the engine for a wave-off it might quit altogether. They said they understood.

Thompson never found him. But somehow Gibby's plane limped along so that he made it back to the ship. He followed procedure and came in for a landing. The signal officer gave him a wave-off!

Court-martial be damned! He cut the gun and dropped to the deck. It was a rough landing, but it was better than winding up in the water! And though he expected a tongue-lashing from the brass, he didn't hear a word.

Almost every afternoon, Kamikazes appeared over the fleet. They would always circle the ships before making their last dive, and this was their undoing. It gave the anti-aircraft a chance to zero in and they would hit the Kamikaze, which would spin downward leaving a trail of smoke.

One of the personnel officers was an old movie star who owned a tennis club in Palm Springs, California. He was friendly with Navy brass who visited his club, and he told them that he wanted to do his bit in the war. They wrangled him a commission and a job on the ***Hornet***, where he spent his time in the sickbay with the doctor, drinking shots of brandy that were meant for pilots after a tough mission. Anyway, when the Kamikazes appeared, the drunken old actor would run out onto the deck, pointing to the sky and announcing their presence.

A significant part of the day occurred when the airmen gathered in the wardroom for dinner. This was time to catch up on the scuttlebutt and get a sense of the general mood, like when a family gathers around the table for the evening meal. The parties at each table knew each other fairly well; the seating was pretty much the same each day. If there had been an important skirmish of some kind, this was the time to hear about it, replete with details. If nothing had happened, there would be casual conversation.

One thing Gibby realized, after many, many of these pre-dinner gatherings, was that he had never once heard a patriotic word. He had seen a boatload of war movies and knew how, when the warriors gather, there was plenty of heroic thought, sometimes subtly stated, but always present. But here, in actual combat conditions, there was not so much as: "Let's go get those Japs!" Instead, there was likely to be an officer scribbling on a napkin, figuring what his flight pay was going to be, now that he had downed two more planes.

Patriotism was something these guys didn't indulge in. They left that for the movies.

But there were rumors. Like, in certain fighter groups, where the leader was regular Navy and outranked the wingmen. The leader claimed all the planes that were shot down by his flight, especially if there was any controversy. His rationale was simple, if self-serving. He was regular Navy; the Navy was his job. Kills were extremely important to him—they figured in his take-home pay, as well as his chance for advancement. The wingmen were reserves, who would go on to another job when the war was over.

The days went on. The night-fighters patrolled the fleet every other night and sometimes went on intruder missions, bombing and strafing small islands that had been bypassed by the retreating Japanese.

One night Gibby was in his plane on the catapult, when off to his right flares began dropping from the sky. They came down in a straight line parallel to the ship. In a few moments the **Hornet** was sailing alongside a curtain of light, as if it were on a stage. It was a tactic they'd heard about. A plane drops a screen of flares on one side of the ship, so that the ship presents a perfect silhouette for the torpedo plane on the other side to launch a missile.

A catapult officer rushed up to the left side of the cockpit. "Get out!" he yelled. "We're gonna take a torpedo!"

"No! No!" said Gibby, unsure. "I don't have orders . . . Get under something. Protect yourself." The officer threw up his hands and vanished. Gibby waited. The whole ship waited for the explosion. But it never came. Later they heard that the first plane had dropped his flares on the wrong side of the ship and blinded the torpedo pilot. Such is war. The side that fucks up least, wins.

Chapter Eighteen 79

Chapter Nineteen

They were at a movie on the hangar deck when they heard a plane overhead. A moment later there was a tremendous explosion and the ship rocked so that the audience was thrown to the left, and then back to the right. Through the open hangar door they saw a mountain of flame, which was the *Bennington*, sailing next to them. A Kamikaze had dived into it and hit the ammo storage. It was the fourth of July! Flaming rockets zoomed in all directions, bombs exploded, flares shot into the sky. It was a stunning sight, and there was bedlam on the *Hornet*. The hangar door was slammed shut, General Quarters was sounded. A voice on the loudspeaker ordered everyone to their rooms, and to stay off the deck. There was no help for the *Bennington*. It burned throughout the night.

But the next morning, it was still there, sailing proudly, but sadly, alongside the *Hornet*. Blackened, scorched, but upright. The firefighters, bravest of the brave, had vanquished the flames and saved the ship. The firefighters were a magnificent bunch. In their white suits and headpieces, they would wade directly into the most ferocious fires to save a pilot who had crashed, or put out a gasoline fire on the deck.

On the hangar deck was a scoreboard of sorts, the kind of scoreboard that was often seen during the war, a collection of decals, miniature enemy flags, each representing a "Kill," a Japanese plane shot down. The pilots of the *Hornet* were responsible for something over four hundred, a matter of great pride among the officers and crew. It was the second highest score in the Navy. But it was also representative of four hundred death agonies, and gallons of blood.

They had been at sea for four-and-a-half months. The ship's crew had been out for almost two years. A strong swell of homesickness engulfed the Hornet, but there seemed no indication of an end to the cruise. Then nature intervened. Reports of a gigantic hurricane came over the radio, and then radar began to pick up the storm itself. There were furious preparations. Planes on deck were lashed down with ropes two inches thick. The phrase: "Batten down the Hatches" was put into practice throughout the ship.

And then it hit. The immense ship was tossed around like a cork. No one could walk in the passageways without getting banged into the walls. Crashes and smashes came from the galley. Word was that the cooks and waiters were throwing china against the walls, hoping that enough damage would speed the ship toward home.

When it was over, people roamed the ship, inspecting the ruin. It was extensive. Furniture was broken, debris filled the rooms. Up on deck the two-inch ropes had torn apart sending planes into each other and some had gone over the side. But the most unbelievable destruction was to the front of the flight deck. Eighteen inches of solid steel had been bent down like a rug over the bow. The flight deck, one hundred and fifty feet above the sea, had plunged so far underwater, the weight of the water had bent the deck when the ship came up.

Joy was in the hearts of the observers of this devastation, and if it hadn't seemed inappropriate to cheer they would have done so, since this looked like a ticket back home. But no orders were received to return stateside. The engineers inspected the bow, trying to determine if the turbulence coming over the twisted metal made it unsafe to launch planes.

The ship, a week or so before, had picked up a Marine pilot who had ditched his plane in the sea. And somebody had an idea. The Marine could be the guinea pig. They told the guy they would give him an airplane and directions to his base. Then they turned the ship into the wind and launched him off the flight deck. He went over the bow, did a slow-roll and dived upside-down into the sea. After they fished him out and apologized, they went into a conference. The Navy officers were not quite satisfied. After all, the guy was only a Marine—what could you expect? Our own carrier pilots could take off with no problem, they were sure.

Four pilots were tagged for the experiment, Gibby among them. They were advised to hold the brakes and give the engine full power before starting their takeoff, then pull up before getting to the end of the deck. The four made their takeoffs successfully. But the brass was still not convinced. The solution, they decided, was to run the ship backward and take off from the rear. This was done for a week or so, and then the orders came to return home.

Chapter Nineteen   **81**

Delight knew no bounds. As the ship turned southwest, the senior pilots decided to hold several extra explorations into the gunnysack to keep everyone in a good mood on the way back.

Chapter Twenty

There was cheering on the flight deck at dusk. Guys who made it up there found other guys pointing straight ahead. Tiny lights were showing—Hawaii! They docked at Pearl Harbor the next morning and Gibby rushed to a phone. He called Della, who could hardly speak, so relieved was she to hear that he was still alive. They met at a restaurant at an outdoor table where birds vied for crumbs while they ate.

"I woke up one night and it was like there was a big bump. Did something happen?"

"Well, I had a bad landing one night . . ."

"Then that was it. I knew it was you." Della had always claimed she was psychic.

"How's Ma?"

"O.K. She's got a job at Marshall Fields."

"Boy, workers must be scarce."

"Yeah. She's dusting furniture in the furniture department."

He laughed. "And how're you?"

"Fine."

"Any boyfriends?"

"No. I'm resigned to dying an old maid."

He had to get back to the ship. They hugged and said goodbye. Very early on a Sunday morning they passed under the Bay Bridge. There were a couple of lone pedestrians looking down at them, probably wondering what had happened to the great ship. They docked at Alameda and were on the loose for a couple of days before going home.

That evening, Gibby was walking along a street in town, a bit smashed, when he ran into Lt. Weathers, also slightly drunk, but glad to see him. "Listen," said the radar officer, "I've got to tell you something. When we were out there, we had a kind of pool—about who was going to make it back and who wasn't."

"Yeah?"

"Yeah. And most of the money was on you."

"To make it back?"

"Guess again."

They laughed heartily. "I hope you didn't lose too much," said Gibby.

"Don't worry about it. It was a pleasure."

They waved at each other as they made their separate way down the street.

March 19, 1962

Dear Stanley:

You haven't heard ffom me because I was visited by another attack of influenza (or its little brother). Chicago has had its worst winter in all history and that's been tough on frail flowers of advanced years like myself. However, I feel today that I may recover. This latest bout with illness has been highlighted by a reactivation of my norally, should be normally, dormant hemorrhoids. Massive doses of something called, I believe, Stereomycin occasioned astonishingly frequent bathroom summonses which threw my posterior machinery into a state of imbalance. My piles are the itching variety and when I venture out on the street I'm apt to walk more and more rapidly until I'm travelling at a dead run. Also I have a tendency to jump over fire hydrants and yelp little nervous yelps. The snapshot above supplies a notion of how a person feels when his hemorrhoids are itching.

❖ ❖ ❖

The next morning the pilots were assembled in the auditorium at the Naval Air Base. Half of them were asleep. Many had vomit on their uniforms. They were slouched, eyes closed, like sacks in their theater seats. Down the aisle came a Chief Petty Officer. He had a cigar box in one hand and a list in the other. He would announce, "Ensign So-and-so, Silver Star, Lt. J.G. So-and-so, Air Medal . . ." As he called the names, he would dig in the cigar box, take out the medal and look around for the recipient. Somebody who was still awake would point him out and the Chief would toss it his way, sometimes caught by a guy next to him. And so it went, until the Chief ran out of medals. Gibby got a DFC and an Air Medal with three stars. "Stub" was poking him in the arm with his elbow.

"Y'know something?"

"What?" asked Gibby.

"Stub" was pretty smashed. "You guys won the war . . ."

"Huh?"

"You guys won the war."

"Who?"

"You and Mac and Burton, and . . . and Thompson . . ."

"What'd ya mean?"

"You guys found all the planes, and the other guys destroyed 'em. That won the war."

"Hey, tell the Admiral, will you?"

"Okay."

The Chief had turned around at the front of the auditorium. He said, "Listen, we got reporters at the back of the room. They're from most of the big cities—Detroit, Kansas City, New York, *Times, Chicago Tribune* . . . So, if you're from one of those places and want to talk to 'em . . . They'll be glad to hear from you, especially if you've had any interesting experiences. If you want the folks back home to know what a big hero you are . . . this is the time to tell your story . . ."

God, Gibby could see the lead line on the entertainment page of the *Chicago Tribune*: "Radio star gets medals in the Pacific." He could get laid from now on. He had stories to tell, and pretty good ones. The reporter would eat it up. But he sat there and didn't move. "You dummy," he raged in his mind. "If you don't go back there and talk to the guy, you'll regret it for the rest of your life!" Still, he sat there.

The truth was, he wasn't happy with what he'd done. If anything, he was ashamed. He knew how they'd write it—make him into a hero. Exciting, dramatic, glamorous. But his sense of truth was troubled. It was all bullshit! So what? Play the game, dummy! Give 'em what they want—fulfill the expectation. But he knew in his heart how it had really been: Senseless, barbaric, and unutterably cruel. He'd killed people, people he would never know, burned them alive, for Christ sake! Of course, he had been trained, brainwashed, and when the time came, just did what he'd been taught to do, automatically, without thought. But it was nothing to be proud of. He got up and walked out.

Chapter Twenty-One

He was home, on thirty days leave. The city looked like heaven, a place he never dreamed he would see again. His mother was back in her old apartment, and beside herself to have him home.

Somehow, Mary and her mother found out he was back. They called and said they'd meet him at Roscoe's, one of their old haunts. When he arrived at the bar, he found there was an additional person in the party—Jack, who was obviously gay and was introduced as Mary's husband.

Jack was a pleasant guy, slightly plump, ingratiating, and very curious about Gibby's friends, especially the women. "Jack designs hats," said Viola. "He's looking for customers. He really makes great hats."

"Do you know anyone who might be interested?" Jack wanted to know.

"I don't. But I'll think about it."

"I'd be so grateful."

"Sure." Gibby took a long look at Mary. She was beautiful as ever.

"How's your life?" he asked her.

"Fine," she said. "It's good to see you."

"We live in a little place on the Kankakee river," said Jack. "We'd love to have you come out."

"Why not? I've got nothing to do for the next thirty days except bum around."

"Great," said Mary. "Here, I'll draw you a map. And give you our phone number."

They had a few drinks and then Gibby excused himself. He put the map in his pocket.

It was time to go to NBC and look in on his old colleagues. He wore his "Greens" because his civvies were still packed. Walking along the corridor toward the studio, he got a vicious kick in the rump, and turned to see an old friend and fellow actor, Art Thurlow, walking with another guy Gibby didn't know. "Hey, Art!" cried Gibby with a laugh, because he wasn't really sure how to react. He put out his hand and Art took it, but with a strange look on his face. There was little warmth there; maybe even a slight hostility. And so the returning vet got his first introduction to the dubious welcome he might receive in the future.

He waited at the door of Studio F, until the red light went off, then went in. Bert and Jeanette were seated at a table, putting their scripts together; a teenage boy was sitting on the couch. Wayne was in the control room with Leonard Jacobs, the director. Jeanette saw him first, came over and hugged him, making little happy, emotional sounds. Bert was right behind, to shake his hand. Meanwhile, Wayne and Leonard were coming in. They introduced the kid on the couch, Marvin Teitelbaum, who had been doing Gibby's part while he was gone. It was a warm, affectionate reunion.

But, it was funny. Gibby was wearing his ribbons, yet there was not one question about where he'd been, or what he'd done. It was as if none of it mattered, as if it wasn't worth talking about. Gibby wasn't all that anxious to talk about it either, yet he felt a small pang of disappointment.

Leonard was on the phone. When he got off, he said, "I called **Radio Guide**. They want to come over tomorrow morning at eleven, and take some pictures. That okay, Gibby?"

"Sure."

"Great."

The next morning, Gibby overslept. And though he tried not to confess it to himself, it was somewhat on purpose. His sense of truth, intruding, forced him to realize he was miffed that they hadn't given him an opportunity to play the hero, and he was paying them back. He watched the clock, with his head on the pillow and saw it crawl toward eleven. The phone rang. It was Wayne, sounding slightly irritated.

"Are you still in bed?"

"Yeah. I overslept."

"Hell, we've all been waiting . . ."

"I'm sorry. Should I come down now?"

"No, they can't stay around."

"I'm sorry."

"Oh . . . That's O.K." Wayne hung up, leaving Gibby to wonder about himself.

He called Mary, and asked if he could come out. "Sure," she said. "When?"

"How about now? I've got nothing to do."

"Great. We'll be waiting for you."

He knew the area somewhat, having hunted rabbits around there in the old days. When he got to the river, he consulted the map. Boy, they were really hiding out.

The house was tiny, back in the trees, at the edge of the river. Gibby parked the car, picked up the bottle of bourbon from the seat, went to the front door and knocked. Mary opened the door and gave him a quick hug and kiss. She was still in her pajamas. There was only a small kitchen, a cramped living room and a bedroom that he couldn't see at the moment.

"Where's Jack?"

"He's in there," pointing to the bedroom. "Working."

"But then Jack appeared, wearing bedroom slippers, no shirt and a floppy black straw hat with a white feather and pink flowers around the brim.

"Hey, Gibby! How ya doin', Man?"

"Good. You're lookin' gorgeous."

Jack hugged him affectionately, almost losing the hat. "Whatd'ya think of the place?"

"I like it."

"Yeah. See, we got a cot over there. You can stay overnight, if you want."

"It depends on how drunk I get." Gibby handed him the bottle.

"Ooh, thank you. How thoughtful."

They had a drink, and then another. Gibby looked at Mary. She smiled at him.

"Y'know," said Jack, "I ought to go in and work some more on the hats. I'm working on one that's really cute."

"Sure, go ahead."

"Why don't you guys take a walk?" He went into the bedroom. Mary and Gibby sat there for a few moments. "It's really pretty out there."

"Let's go," said Gibby.

They went outside and down to the river. It moved slowly, brown and mysterious. "I wonder if they're any fish in there?"

"I don't think I'd eat any, even if there were."

They walked along the bank, then Mary led the way around the back of the house into the woods. It felt like they were all alone in the world, silent except for the occasional call of a bird. They held hands as they walked. After a few moments, Gibby stopped. She came into his arms.

They sank to the ground, into the lush foliage. She gave a little moan. They kissed as if they were starving and wandered onto a banquet. He pulled down the bottoms of her pajamas with her help. It was unreal, as if they were on another plane. The world fell away from them, and they were weightless, moving in a vacuum. When they got back to the house, Jack was still in the bedroom. But when he heard the door he came out.

"Hey, how was the walk?"

"Good," said Gibby.

"Beautiful," said Mary. "Is anybody hungry?"

"Got any cereal?" said Jack. "I wouldn't mind some cereal . . ." "Captain Crunch," said Mary.

"Great. Want some Captain Crunch, Gibby?"

"Why not?"

They had Captain Crunch and then more bourbon, and a lot of laughs, until it was time to go to bed.

"I hope you'll be comfortable out here," said Mary.

"I'll be fine," said Gibby.

The cot was comfortable, but Gibby couldn't sleep. He could only think about Mary. What a fool he'd been all these years. He wasn't going to sleep, he knew that. Finally he got up and moved slowly to the bedroom. It was pitch black, but he could hear them breathing deeply. There were two dark mounds in the bed. The nearest one was Mary, he was certain. He carefully slid in beside her. Oops, it was Jack.

Carefully, carefully, he got back out and tiptoed around to the other side. He got in and lay there, his heart pounding. She stirred and turned onto her back. He reached out his hand and put it on her stomach, low down. After a long moment, she put her hand on his. They lay that way as minutes passed. He could feel her heart pounding along with his. He reached up to her breast. After a time she covered his hand. He took her hand and moved it to his cock. She squeezed it gently. They didn't move. Then suddenly Mary sat up and got out of bed. Puzzled, he continued to lie there, half expecting her to return. She didn't.

He got out of bed and went back to the living room. She was lying on the cot, on top of the covers. He lay down beside her. Her lips were hot as she kissed him. They explored each other hungrily, doing all the things they'd ached to do in the years gone by. Finally she got up and went back into the bedroom.

"I've got three eggs," she said from the kitchen, as Gibby and Jack sat sleepily at the table in the living room. "I could scramble them with a little milk . . ."

"Got any bread?" asked Jack.

"Yeah, it's not bad. I cut out the moldy part."

"O.K. Is there any coffee?"

"A little."

"Great."

"I'll just have coffee," said Gibby. "Half a cup is fine."

Jack leaned toward Gibby. "I hope you'll come out once in a while." He paused. "And if you and Mary want to go for a walk, that's O.K."

Pretty soon Mary came in with the scrambled eggs and coffee, and sat down with them.

"How are you guys getting along?" asked Gibby.

"What do you mean?" said Mary.

"Well, you seem kind of low on food."

"We're on food stamps. But we ran out. We get some more day after tomorrow."

"What do you do until then? Eat grass?" They laughed.

"Naw, there's always something. Last month we ate vanilla wafers for almost a week."

They finished breakfast and Gibby said he had to go. He hugged them both and then dropped a few bills on the table. They complained weakly, but he ran out the door and closed it quickly behind him.

On his way back to the apartment, he stopped in at the Elk's Club in Oak Park, and found that his father had already arrived, and was sleeping peacefully in his favorite easychair. Gibby sat down in the chair next to him and put his hand on the old man's arm. Ben jerked spasmodically and came awake. Then took a minute or two to recognize who was sitting next to him. "Gibby . . ."

"Yeah, Dad."

They went through the normal questions and answers about when, where, and the state of each other's health, then his father said: "Gibby, what did you do in the war, exactly?"

"I flew airplanes, Dad."

His father nodded. "I see." There was a pause, and then the old man said, "So you never rode a mule at all?"

Chapter Twenty-Two

His mother was upset about his being gone all night, but he told her he'd gone to visit a pal from the Navy and had stayed over. She still groused that he hadn't called. "Listen, Ma, I was gone for almost a year and you didn't know where I was . . ."

"Yeah, yeah. Oh, I forgot—Mr. Geller called yesterday. Call him back."

He called, and Geller asked if Gibby could come in and see him. "Sure."

He was sitting in a leather chair opposite the executive, who was behind his desk.

"I've got some bad news," said Bill.

"Yeah? What?"

"They're canceling the show."

"You're kidding."

"No. The ratings have tanked. They started going down after you left."

"Oh, God. It's my fault, huh?"

"Well, nobody is going to blame you. It was an act of God. But if you remember, I tried to tell you . . ."

"I know, I know . . ."

Geller sat there, his elbows on the desk, his chin on his fists. Staring sympathetically at Gibby, "I'm sorry . . ."

"Oh, hell. When are they gonna pull the plug?"

"In two weeks."

"Um. They were gonna write me in, in two weeks."

"Probably won't happen now. But listen, could I give you a little advice . . . ?"

"Sure."

"Things are different now. I don't know if you're aware, but radio has left Chicago. It's on both coasts now—New York and L.A. Before the war, Chicago was the center of everything, because there were no transcontinental broadcasts. We did a show for one coast and another show for the other—Red and Blue networks. Now they don't need Chicago."

"So if I want to work, I've got to go to New York or L.A. . . ."

"Probably."

Gibby took a deep breath.

"It's tough, but that's the way it is."

Gibby shook hands with the executive and left. He took the elevator down to the lobby, thinking this would probably be the last time he did this, after so many years. He went outside and stood on the sidewalk, looking around at the city, the city that was no longer his home. He would have to start over—as a man; when he had left, he was a boy. He had thought the transition would be from war to peace, but it was going to be a lot more than that. He felt suddenly helpless. No one knew him as a man, only as a kid. It was strange but he wasn't sure he could act like a man—portray a man. In a place he had never lived before. He had no friends in New York or L.A. He had no career, really. He would start from the beginning, and there was probably no one less welcome than a child actor out of work. He began walking to his car.

When he got back to the apartment, his mother said, "You got a telegram." She reached into her bowl of yarn and took it out. Gibby opened it and read:

"WAYNE DIED PEACEFULLY LAST NIGHT. FUNERAL AT GRACELAND CHAPEL, THURSDAY 2:30.

FROM CARROLS 25 EAST ERIE.

LOVE, MARY FRANCIS.

Gibby—with his squad in operational training. Gibby is last one on right, kneeling.

Chapter Twenty-Two

www.ingramcontent.com/pod-product-compliance
Lightning Source LLC
Chambersburg PA
CBHW031643170426
43195CB00035B/567